Famous Hu~~~~
of History

By
ALBERT PAYSON TERHUNE

THE WORLD PUBLISHING COMPANY

CLEVELAND AND NEW YORK

Published by THE WORLD PUBLISHING COMPANY

2231 WEST 110TH STREET · CLEVELAND · OHIO

TOWER BOOKS EDITION

FIRST PRINTING MAY 1943
SECOND PRINTING JULY 1943

FOREWORD

Find the Woman.

You will discover her in almost every generation, in almost every country, in almost every big city—the Super-Woman. She is not the typical adventuress; she is not a genius. The reason for her strange power is occult. When psycho-vivisectionists have thought they had segregated the cause—the formula—what you will—in one particular Super-Woman or group of Super-Women, straightway some new member of the clan has arisen who wields equal power with her notable sisters, but who has none of the traits that made them irresistible. And the seekers of formulas are again at sea.

What makes the Super-Woman? Is it beauty? Cleopatra and Rachel were homely. Is it daintiness? Marguerite de Valois washed her hands but twice a week. Is it wit? Pompadour and La Valliere were avowedly stupid in conversation. Is it youth? Diane de Poictiers and Ninon de l'Enclos were wildly adored at sixty. Is it the subtle quality of femininity? George Sand, who numbered her admirers by the score—poor Chopin in their foremost rank—was not only ugly, but disgustingly mannish. So was Semiramis.

The nameless charm is found almost as often in the masculine, "advanced" woman as in the ultrafeminine damsel.

Here are stories of Super-Women who conquered at will.   Some of them smashed thrones; some were content with wholesale heart-smashing.   Wherein lay their secret?   Or, rather, their secrets?   For seldom did two of them follow the same plan of campaign.

ALBERT PAYSON TERHUNE

"Sunnybank,"
    Pompton Lakes,
        New Jersey

CONTENTS

FAMOUS HUSSIES
OF HISTORY

CHAPTER ONE

LOLA MONTEZ

THE DANCER WHO KICKED OVER A THRONE

H ER MAJESTY'S Theatre in London, one night
in 1843, was jammed from pit to roof. Lumley
the astute manager, had whispered that he had
a "find." His whisper had been judiciously pitched in
a key that enabled it to penetrate St. James Street
clubs, Park Lane boudoirs, even City counting-rooms.

The managerial whisper had been augmented by a
"private view," to which many journalists and a few
influential men about town had been bidden. These
lucky guests had shifted the pitch from whisper to
pæan. By word of mouth and by ardent quill the
song of praise had spread. One of the latter forms of
tribute had run much in this rural-newspaper form:

"A brilliant **divertissement** is promised by Mr. Lumley for the forthcoming performance of 'The Tarantula,'
at Her Majesty's. Thursday evening will mark the
British debut of the mysterious and bewitchingly beautiful Castilian dancer, Lola Montez.

"Through the delicate veins of this lovely daughter
of dreamy Andalusia sparkles the **sang azur** which is

the birthright of the hidalgo families alone. In her is embodied not alone the haughty lineage of centuries of noble ancestry, but all the fire and mystic charm that are the precious heritage of the Southland.

"At a private view, yesterday, at which your correspondent had the honor to be an invited guest, this peerless priestess of Terpsichore——"

And so on for well-nigh a column of adjective-starred panegyric, which waxed more impassioned as the dictionary's supply of unrepeated superlatives waned. This was before the day of the recognized press agent. Folk had a way of believing what they read. Hence the gratifyingly packed theater to witness the mysterious Spaniard's debut.

Royalty itself, surrounded by tired gentlemen in waiting who wanted to sit down and could not, occupied one stage box. In the front of another, lolled Lord Ranelagh, arbiter of London fashion and accepted authority on all matters of taste—whether in dress, dancers, or duels. Ranelagh, recently come back from a tour of the East, divided with royalty the reverent attention of the stalls.

The pit whistled and clapped in merry impatience for the appearance of the danseuse. The West End section of the house waited in equal, if more subdued eagerness, and prepared to follow every possible expression of Ranelagh's large-toothed, side-whiskered visage as a signal for its own approval or censure of the much-advertised Lola's performance.

The first scene of the opera passed almost un-noticed. Then the stage was cleared and a tense hush gripped the house. A fanfare of cornets; and from the wings a supple, dark girl bounded.

A whirlwind of welcome from pit and gallery greeted her. She struck a sensuous pose in the stage's exact center. The cornetists laid aside their instruments.

Guitars and mandolins set up a throbby string overture. Lola drew a deep breath, flashed a vivid Spanish smile on the audience at large, and took the first languid step of her dance.

Then it was that the dutiful signal seekers cast covert looks once more at Lord Ranelagh. That ordinarily stolid nobleman was leaning far forward in his stage box, mouth and eyes wide, staring with incredulous amaze at the posturing Andalusian. Before her first step was complete, Ranelagh's astonishment burst the shackles of silence.

"Gad!" he roared, his excited voice smashing through the soft music and penetrating to every cranny. "Gad! It's little Betty James!"

He broke into a Homeric guffaw. A toady who sat beside him hissed sharply. The hiss and the guf-faw were cues quite strong enough for the rest of the house. A sizzling, swishing chorus of hisses went up from the stalls. was caught by the pit, and tossed aloft in swelling crescendo to the gallery, where it was in-tensified to treble volume.

Lola's artistically made-up face had gone white

under its rouge and pearl powder at Ranelagh's shout. Now it flamed crimson. The girl danced on; she was gallant, a thoroughbred to the core—even though she chanced to be thoroughbred Irish instead of thorough-bred Spanish—and she would not be hissed from the stage.

But now "boos" mingled with the hisses. And Ranelagh's immoderate laughter was caught up by scores of people who did not in the least know at what they were laughing.

The storm was too heavy to weather. Lumley growled an order. Down swooped the curtain, leaving the crowd booing on one side of it, and Lola raging on the other.

Which ended the one and only English theatrical experience of Lola Montez, the dreamy Andalusian dancer from County Limerick, Ireland. That night at Almack's, Lord Ranelagh told a somewhat lengthy story—a story whose details he had picked up in the East—which was repeated with interesting variations next day on Rotten Row, in a dozen clubs, in a hundred drawing rooms. There is the gist of the tale:

Some quarter century before the night of Lola's London **premiere**—and **derniere**—an Irish girl, Eliza Oliver by name, had caught the errant fancy of a great man. The man chanced to be Lord Byron, at that time loafing about the Continent and trying, outwardly at least, to live up to the mental image of himself that was just then enshrined in the hearts of several thousand demure English schoolmaids.

Byron soon tired of Miss Oliver—it is doubtful whether he ever saw her daughter—and the Irish beauty soon afterward married a fellow countryman of her own—Sir Edward Gilbert, an army captain.

The couple's acquaintances being overmuch given to prattling about things best forgotten, Gilbert exchanged to a regiment in India, taking along his wife and her little girl. The child had meantime been christened Maria Dolores Eliza Rosanna; which, for practical purposes, was blue-penciled down to "Betty."

Seven years afterward, Gilbert died. His widow promptly married Captain Craigie, a solid, worthy, Scotch comrade-at-arms of her late husband's. Craigie generously assumed all post-Byronic responsibilities, along with the marriage vows. And, at his expense, Betty was sent to Scotland—later to Paris—to be educated.

At sixteen the girl was a beauty—and a witch as well. She and her mother spent a season at Bath, a resort that still retained in those days some shreds of its former glory. And there—among a score of younger and poorer admirers—two men sued for Betty's hand.

One was Captain James, a likable, susceptible, not over-clever army officer, home on furlough from India. The other was a judge, very old, very gouty, very rich.

And Betty's mother chose the judge, out of all the

train of suitors, as her son-in-law-elect. Years had taught worldly wisdom to the once-gay Eliza.

Betty listened in horror to the old man's mumbled vows. Then, at top speed, she fled to Captain James. She told James that her mother was seeking to sacrifice her on the altar of wealth. James, like a true early-Victorian hero, rose manfully to the occasion.

He and Betty eloped, were married by a registrar, and took the next out-bound ship for India.

It was a day of long and slow voyages. Betty beguiled the time on shipboard by a course of behavior such as would have prevented the most charitable fellow passenger from mistaking her for a returning missionary.

There were many Anglo-Indians—officers and civilians—aboard. And Betty's flirtations, with all and sundry, speedily became the scandal of the ship. By the time the vessel docked in India, there were dozens of women ready to spread abroad the bride's fame in her new home land.

English society in India was, and is, in many respects like that of a provincial town. In the official and army set, one member's business is everybody's business.

Nor did Betty take any pains to erase the impressions made by her volunteer advance agents. Like a blazing star, she burst upon the horizon of India army life. Gloriously beautiful, willful, capricious, brilliant, she speedily had a horde of men at her feet—and a still larger number of women at her throat.

Her flirtations were the talk of mess-room and bungalow. Heartlessly, she danced on hearts. There was some subtle quality about her that drove men mad with infatuation.

And her husband? He looked on in horrified wonder. Then he argued and even threatened. At last he shut up and took to drink. Betty wrote contemptuously to a friend, concerning this last phase:

"He spends his time in drinking, and then in sleeping like a gorged boa-constrictor."

James was liked by the English out there, and his friends fiercely resented the domestic treatment that was turning a popular and promising officer into a sodden beast.

One morning James rode away over the hills and neglected to come back. His wife never again heard of him. And at his exit from the scene, the storm broke; a storm of resentment that swept Betty James out beyond even the uttermost fringe of Anglo-Indian society.

She hunted up her generous old step-father, Craigie, and induced him to give her a check for a thousand pounds, to get rid of her forever. She realized another thousand on her votive offerings of jewelry; and, with this capital, she took the dust of India from her pretty slippers.

Here ends Lord Ranelagh's scurrilous narrative, told at Almack's.

On her way back to England, Betty broke her journey at Spain, remaining there long enough to acquire three valuable assets—a Spanish accent, a semitolerable knowledge of Spanish dancing, and the ultra-Spanish name of Lola Montez, by which—through mere courtesy to her wishes—let us hereafter call her. Then she burst upon the British public—only to retire amid a salvo of hisses and catcalls.

With the permature fall of the curtain at Her Majesty's Theater. begins the Odyssey of Lola Montez.

She went from London to Germany, where she danced for a time, to but scant applause, at second-rate theaters, and at last could get no more engagements.

Thence she drifted to Brussels, where, according to her own later statement. she was "reduced to singing in the streets to keep from starving." Contemporary malice gives a less creditable version of her means of livelihood in the Belgian capital. It was a period of her life—the black hour before the garish dawn—of which she never afterward would talk.

But before long she was on the stage again: this time at Warsaw. during a revolution. She danced badly and was hissed. But the experience gave her an idea.

She went straightway to Paris, where, by posing as an exiled Polish patriot, she secured an engagement at the Porte St. Martin Theater. It was her last hope.

The "Polish patriot" story brought a goodly crowd to Lola's first performance in Paris. But, after a single dance, she heard the horribly familiar sound of hisses.

And at the first hiss, her Irish spirit blazed into a crazy rage; a rage that was the turning point of her career.

Glaring first at the spectators like an angry cat, Lola next glared around the stage for a weapon wherewith to wreak her fury upon them. But the stage was bare.

Frantic, she kicked off her slippers, and then tore loose her heavy-buckled garters. With these intimate missiles she proceeded to pelt the grinning occupants of the front row, accompanying the volley with a high-pitched, venomous Billingsgate tirade in three languages.

That was enough. On the instant the hisses were drowned in a salvo of applause that shook the rafters. Lola Montez had "arrived." Paris grabbed her to its big, childish, fickle heart.

She was a spitfire and she couldn't dance. But she had given the Parisians a genuine thrill. She was a success. Two slippers and two garters, hurled with feminine rage and feminine inaccuracy into the faces of a line of bored theatergoers, had achieved more for the fair artillerist than the most exquisite dancing could have hoped to.

Lola was the talk of the hour.   An army of babbling Ranelaghs could not now have dimmed her fame.

Dujarrier, all-powerful editor of "La Presse," laid his somewhat shopworn heart at her feet.   Dumas, Balzac, and many another celebrity sued for her favor. Her reign over the hearts of men had recommenced.

But Lola Montez never rode long on prosperity's wave-crest.   A French adorer, jealous of Dujarrier's prestige with the lovely dancer, challenged the great editor to a duel.   Dujarrier, for love of Lola, accepted the challenge—and was borne off the field of honor with a bullet through his brain.

Lola sought to improve the occasion by swathing herself somberly and right becomingly in crape, and by vowing a vendetta against the slayer.   But before she could profit by the excellent advertisement, Dumas chanced to say something to a friend—who repeated it to another friend, who repeated it to all Paris—that set the superstitious, mid-century Frenchmen to looking askance at Lola and to avoiding her gaze.   Said Monte Cristo's creator:

"She has the evil eye.   She will bring a curse upon any man who loves her."

And by that (perhaps) senseless speech, Dumas drove Lola Montez from Paris.   But she took with her all her newborn prestige as a danseuse.   She took it first to Berlin.   There she was bidden to dance at a court reception tendered by King Frederick William, of Prussia.

The rooms of the palace, on the night of the reception, were stiflingly hot. Lola asked for a glass of water. A much-belaced and bechained chamberlain— to whom the request was repeated by a footman—sent word to Lola that she was there to dance for the king and not to order her fellow-servants around.

The net result of this answer was another Irish rage. Lola, regardless of her pompous surroundings, rushed up to the offending chamberlain and loudly made known her exact opinion of him. She added that she was tired of dealing with understrappers, and that, unless the king himself would bring her a glass of water, there would be no dreamy Spanish dance at the palace that night.

The scandalized officials moved forward in a body to hustle the **lesemajeste** perpetrator out of the sacred precincts. But the rumpus had reached the ears of King Frederick William himself, at the far end of the big room. His majesty came forward in person to learn the cause of the disturbance. He saw a marvelously beautiful woman in a marvelously abusive rage.

To the monarch's amused queries, the chamberlain bleated out the awful, sacrilegious, **schrecklich** tale of Lola's demand. The king did not order her loaded with chains and haled to the donjon keep. Instead, he gave a laughing order—this gracious and gentle sovereign who had so keen an eye for beauty.

A moment later a lackey brought the king a glass of water. First gallantly touching the goblet to his own lips, his majesty handed it with a deep obeisance to Lola.

Except for the advertisement it gave her, she could gain no real advantage from this odd introduction to a king. For, next day, she received a secret, but overwhelmingly official hint that an instant departure not only from Berlin. but from Prussia. too, would be one of the wisest moves in her whole career. She went.

To Bavaria, and to greatness.

Lola Montez, the Spanish dancer, was billed at a Munich theater. She danced there but three times. For, on the third evening, the royal box was occupied by a drowsy-eyed sexagenarian whose uniform coat was ablaze with decorations.

The old gentleman was Ludwig I. **Dei gratia,** King of Bavaria, a ruler who up to this time had been beloved of his subjects; and whose worst vice, in his people's eyes, was that he encouraged art rather than arms.

Ludwig watched breathlessly while Lola danced. Afterward he sent for her to come to the royal box and be presented to him. She never danced again in Bavaria.

For next day Ludwig introduced her at court as "my very good friend." Lola dazzled Munich with her jewels and her equipages. The king presented her with a huge and hideous mansion. He stretched the laws by having her declared a Bavarian subject. And, having done that, he bestowed upon her the titles of

"Baroness von Rosenthal and Countess von Landfeld."
Next, he granted her an annuity of twenty thousand
florins. Things were coming Lola's way, and coming
fast.

The Bavarians did not dislike her—at first. When
Ludwig forced his queen to receive her and to pin
upon the dancer-emeritus' breast the Order of St.
Theresa, there was, to be sure, a shocked murmur.
But it soon died down. Had Lola been content
with her luck, she might have continued indefinitely
in her new and delightfully comfortable mode of
life.

But, according to Lola's theory, a mortal who is
content with success would be content with failure.
And she strove to play a greater role than the fat one
assigned to her by the love-sick old king.

She had read of Pompadour and other royal fav-
orites whose vagrom whims swayed the destinies of
Europe. She sought to be a world power; the power
behind the throne; the woman who could mold the
politics of a dynasty. And she laid her plans accordingly.

It was not even a dream, this new ambition of Lola's.
It was a comic-opera fantasy. Bavaria, at best,
was only a little German state with no special
voice in the congress of nations. And Lola herself had no more aptitude for politics than she had
for dancing. Nor did she stop to consider that Ger-
mans in 1846 were much more likely to tolerate a

fair foreigner's meddling with their puppet king's domestic affairs than with matters of public welfare.

But Lola Montez ever did the bulk of her sane thinking when it was too late. So she proceeded to put her idiotic plans into operation.

First, she cajoled King Ludwig into dismissing in a body his perfectly capable and well-liked ministry. As delighted with that success as is the village cut-up when he pulls a chair from under the portly constable—and with even less wholesome fear of the result to herself —Lola next persuaded the king to change his whole policy of state. Then things began to happen.

One morning Lola awoke in her ugly and costly mansion to find the street in front of the door blocked by a highly unfriendly mob, whose immediate ambition seemed to be the destruction of the house and herself. This was the signal for one more Irish rage, the last on public record.

Lola, throwing a wrapper over her nightgown, snatched up a loaded pistol, and, pushing aside her screaming servants, ran out on the front steps.

At sight of her the crowd roared in fury and made a dash for the steps. Lola retaliated by emptying her revolver into the advancing mob. Events had moved rapidly since the primitive days when she was content to bombard her detractors with slippers and garter buckles.

The rioters halted, before the fusillade. Before they could combine for another rush, and while Lola from the topmost step was reviling them in her best and fiercest German, a company of the royal bodyguard, headed by the old king himself, charged through the crowd and rescued the angry woman.

But, though Ludwig had just saved her from a sudden and extremely unpleasant form of death, he was not strong enough to stem the avalanche of public opinion that crashed down upon her. This same avalanche proceeded to brush Lola out of her big and hideous house, to knock away from her her titles of baroness and countess and her twenty-thousand-florin annuity, and to whirl her across the Bavarian frontier with stern instructions never to return.

Incidentally, poor old King Ludwig came in for so much unpopularity on her account that he was forced to abdicate. Thus, in her own fall from power, Lola had also dragged a once-popular king off his throne; a noteworthy achievement, in that pre-Gaby-Deslys period, for an Irish girl with a variegated past.

The Ludwig scandal preceded Lola wherever she tried to go. The divinity that hedges a king was everywhere on guard against her. The gate to practically every country in Europe was slammed in her face. Folk fell to repeating Dumas' "evil-eye" words, and to applying them to discrowned old Ludwig. Lola Montez was not wanted anywhere; certainly nowhere east of the Atlantic.

So she came to New York. Here there were no kings, to bar her out lest they share Ludwig's fate.

And Americans knew little and cared less about the evil eye.   If Lola Montez could make good on the stage, America was willing to welcome her: If not, it had no further general interest in her.

Moreover, she was well past thirty; at an age when the first glory of a woman's siren charms may reasonably be supposed to be slightly blurred.   New Yorkers were curious to see her, on account of her history; but that was their only interest in her.

She danced at the old Broadway Theater.   People thronged the theater for the first few performances. Then, having gazed their fill on the Bavarian throne's wrecker and finding she could not dance, they stayed away; and Lola ended her engagement at the Broadway to the hackneyed "beggarly array of empty benches."

An enterprising manager—P. T. Barnum, if I remember aright—raked up the Byron story and starred Lola in a dramatization of Lord Byron's poem "Mazeppa."   But people here had already looked at her, and the production was a failure.   Next she appeared in one or two miserably written plays, based on her own European adventures.   These, too, failed.   She then wrote a beauty book that had a small sale, and wrote also a drearily stupid volume of humor, designed as a mock "Guide to Courtship."

On her way to America, Lola had stopped in England long enough to captivate and marry a British army officer, Heald by name.   But she soon left him, and arrived in this country without visible matrimonial ties.

New York having tired of her, Lola went West. She created a brief, but lively, furore among the gold-boom towns along the Pacific coast; not so much by reason of her story as for the wondrous charm that was still hers. She gave lectures in California, and then made an Australian tour.

Coming back from the Antipodes, she settled for a time in San Francisco. There, in rather quick succession, she married twice. One of her two California spouses was Hull, the famous pioneer newspaper owner, of San Francisco.

But she quickly wearied of the West, and of her successive husbands. Back she came to New York. And—to the wonder of all, and the incredulity of most—she there announced that, though she had been a great sinner, she was now prepared to devote the rest of her life to penance.

Strangely enough, her new resolve was not a pose. Even in her heyday she had given lavishly to charity. Now she took up rescue work among women. She did much good in a quiet way, spending what money she had on the betterment of her sex's unfortunates, and toiling night and day in their behalf.

Under this unaccustomed mode of life, Lola's health went to pieces. She was sent to a sanitarium in Astoria, L. I. And there, in poverty and half forgotten, she died.   Kindly neighbors scraped together enough money to bury her.

Thus ended in wretched anticlimax the meteor career of Lola Montez; Wonder Woman and wanderer; over-thrower of a dynasty and worse-than-mediocre dancer.   Some one has called her "the last of the great adventuresses."   And that is perhaps her best epitaph.

Her neglected grave—in Greenwood Cemetery, in Brooklyn, by the way—bears no epitaph at all.   That last resting place of a very tired woman is marked merely by a plain headstone, whose dimmed lettering reads:

Mrs. Eliza Gilbert.   Died June 16, 1861.   Age 42.

One trembles to think of the near-royal Irish rage that would have possessed Lola if, at her baroness-countess-Bavarian zenith, she could have foreseen that dreary little postscript to her lurid life missive.

CHAPTER TWO

NINON DE L'ENCLOS

PREMIERE SIREN OF TWO CENTURIES.

THIS story opens with the account of a deathbed scene; somewhat different from any other you may have read. It is brought in to throw a light on what heredity and careful instruction can do in molding a young mind. But don't necessarily skip it for that reason.

One day in 1630, the Sieur de L'Enclos lay dying in his great, dreary bedroom in his great, dreary Touraine castle. There was no especial tragedy about the closing of his life. He was elderly, very rich, and possessed of a record for having used, to the full, every minute of a long and exciting life.

Beside his bed stood a fifteen-year-old girl, his only daughter, Anne; affectionately nicknamed by him— and later by all Europe and still later by all history— "Ninon." She was something below medium height, plump, with a peachblow complexion, huge dark eyes, and a crown of red-gold hair. Ninon and her father had been chums, kindred spirits, from the girl's babyhood.

The dying noble opened his eyes. They rested lovingly on the daughter who had bent down to hear the whispered sounds his white lips were striving to frame. Then, with a mighty effort, De L'Enclos breathed his solemn last words of counsel to the girl —counsel intended to guide her through the future that he knew must lie before so rich and so beautiful a damsel. This was his message to her:

"Ninon—little girl of mine—in dying I have but one single regret. I regret that I did not—get more fun out of life. I warn you—daughter—do not make the terrible mistake that I have made. Live—live so that at the last you will not have the same cause for sorrow!"

So saying, the Sieur de L'Enclos bade an exemplary farewell to earth and to its lost opportunities of fun. To judge from his career as well as from his last words, one may venture the optimistic belief that he had not thrown away as many such priceless chances as he had led his daughter to believe.

Ninon, then, at fifteen, was left alone in the world. And her actions in this sad state conformed to those of the customary helpless orphan—about as closely as had her father's death speech to the customary "last words." With a shrewdness miraculous in so young a girl, she juggled her Touraine property in a series of deals that resulted in its sale at a little more than double its actual value. Rich beyond all fear of want, she settled in Paris.

It was not there or then that her love life set in. That had begun long before. As a mere child she had flashed upon her little world of Touraine as a wonder girl. The superwoman charm was hers from the first. And she retained it in all its mysterious power through the seventeenth century and into the eighteenth; men vying for her love when she was ninety.

A full year before her father died, she had met the youthful Prince de Marsillac, and had, at a glance, wholly captivated his semi-royal fancy. It was Ninon's first love affair—with a prince. She was dazzled by it just a little, she whom monarchs later could not dazzle. She was only fourteen. And in Touraine a princely admirer was a novelty.

At Marsillac's boyish supplication, Ninon consented to elope with him. Off they started. And back to their respective homes they were brought in dire disgrace. There was all sorts of a scandal in the neighborhood. The princeling was soundly spanked and packed off to school. The Sieur de L'Enclos came in for grave popular disapproval by laughingly refusing to mete out the same stern penalties to Ninon.

To Paris, then, at sixteen, went the orphaned Ninon. Laughing at convention and at the threats of her shocked relatives, she set up housekeeping on her own account, managing the affairs of her Rive Gauche mansion with the ease of a fifty-year-old **grande dame.**

On Paris burst the new star. In a month the city

was crazy over her.   Not her beauty alone, nor her
wit, nor her peculiar elegance, nor her incredibly high
spirits.—Not any or all of these, but an all-compelling
magnetism drew men to her in shoals and swarms.

By reason of her birth and breeding she took at
once her place in the court society of the day.   Before
she was twenty, she was setting the fashions for feminine Paris, and was receiving in her salon the state-
liest ladies of the court, in equal numbers with their
far less stately husbands.

Frankly, she declared herself a votary, not of love,
but of loves.   For constancy she had no use what-
soever.   One admirer who had won a temporay lease
of her gay heart swore he would kill himself unless
Ninon would swear to love him to eternity.

And as she loved him ardently, she made the rash
vow.   When at the end of ninety days she gave him
his dismissal, he reproached her wildly and bitterly
for her broken pledge.

"You swore you would love me to eternity!" he
raged.   "And now———"

"And now," she explained, as one might soothe a
cranky child, "I have kept my vow.   I have loved
you for three endless months.   That is an eternity—
for love!"

And three months remained, to the end, Ninon's
record for fidelity to any one man; which was, perhaps, as well, for the waiting list was as long as that
of a hyper-fashionable club.

And now we come to a story that I do not ask you to believe, although all France unquestionably and unquestioningly believed it. Whether Ninon herself at first coined it as a joke, or whether it was a hoax that she herself credited, it is certain that she grew at last to have firm faith in it.

One night—so Ninon always declared—when she was about twenty, she returned home late from a ball at the Hotel St. Evremond. As she stood before the mirror of her boudoir, after her maid had left her for the night, she became aware of a shadowy reflection behind her.

Turning, she saw a man clad all in black, his face hidden by the low brim of his hat and by his cloak's folds. What little was visible of his countenance was ghastly pale. Ninon, ever fearless, did not cry out for help. Instead, she approached the black-shrouded stranger and demanded to know his business and how he had penetrated to her close-barred room.

The man in black, by way of answer, drew one sable-gloved hand from beneath his cloak. In his fingers he grasped a large phial, wherein sparkled and glowed a strange, pinkish liquid.

"Life is short," said the visitor, as Ninon still looked in amazed inquiry from his half-hidden face to the rose-colored phial he carried. "Life is short, but youth is far shorter. When youth is gone, love is gone. Love is the goal of life. Without youth, there is no love. Without love, life is a desert. The gift

of youth and beauty are yours. Would you make
them long-lasting, instead of transient blessings that
shall too soon become mere memories?"

As Ninon, dumb with wonder, hesitated to reply,
he continued:

"The admiration of men melts like summer snow
at the first touch of age in a woman. Their admiration is now yours. Would you hold it? One drop
a day from this phial, in your bath, will keep you
young. will keep you beautiful. will retain for you the
love of men."

He set the flask on her dressing table and turned
to go.

"**You will see me again,**" he said very slowly and
distinctly, "**just three days before your death.**"

And he vanished.

To a generation that has substituted science for
superstition, this tale of the Man in Black reads like
stark nonsense. Perhaps it is. But no one in the
seventeenth century thought so. It was an age rife
with demon legends; legends of favors granted to
mortals in return for a residuary mortgage on their
souls; and all that sort of thing. The tale of Faust
was still almost brand-new. Compared with many of
the traditions that then passed for solid fact, the incident of Ninon and the Man in Black was almost
commonplace.

We laugh at such things; probably with due justi-
fication. Yet was Ninon's adventure more inexplic-

able than some of the absolutely authenticated cases of Cagliostro's magic? As, for a single example, when on a certain date Cagliostro announced in Paris: "The Empress Maria Theresa of Austria died this morning." This was long before the time of telegraphy or even of railroads. It was a journey of several days from Paris to Vienna. Dispatches, reaching the French court a week later, announced the unforeseen death of Maria Theresa at the very hour named by Cagliostro.

Ninon may have invented the Man in Black. Or he may have been one of the many quacks who hung on the fringes of courts and made capital out of the superstitious folly of the rich. Or perhaps——

At all events, seventy years later, Ninon had either a most remarkable encounter with the same man, or else, in her dying moments, she took odd trouble to substantiate a silly lie that was nearly three-quarters of a century old. Finish the story and then form your own theories.

Paris was alive in those days with titled women whose antecedents were doubtful and about whose characters there could unluckily be no doubt. They moved in the best society—or, rather, in the highest. Most of them made a living by one form or another of graft. And always there was an exclusive class of women who would not receive them.

Ninon quickly proved she had neither lot nor parcel with these titled adventuresses. From first to last she accepted not a sou, not a jewel, not a favor—political or otherwise—from the **grands seigneurs** who delighted to do her honor. From first to last, too, she accepted as her due the friendship of the most respectable and respected members of her own sex.

She was never an adventuress, never a grafter, never a climber. She loved for love's own sake. And if the men to whom in lightning succession she gave her resilient heart chanced often to be among the foremost of the realm, it was only because the qualities that made them what they were made them also the type of man Ninon preferred.

She never benefited in any material way from their adoration. The nearest approach was when Richelieu, the grim old iron cardinal, bent his ecclesiastical and consumptive body before her altar. She used her power over Richelieu freely, but never for herself; always to soften the punishment of some luckless man or woman who had fallen under the rod of his eminence's displeasure.

Thereby, and through Richelieu's love for her, Ninon clashed with no less a personage than the Queen of France herself.

When Anne of Austria came from Spain to be the bride of Louis XIII of France, Richelieu fell in love with the pretty young queen. Anne had not wit enough to appreciate the cardinal's genius or to fear his possible hate. So—seeing in him only a homely and emaciated little man, whose pretensions she con-

sidered laughable—the queen hit on a scheme of rid-
ding herself forever of Richelieu's love sighs.

She pretended to listen to his courtship, then told
him coyly that his austerity and lack of human weakness and of humor made her afraid of him. The enamored Richelieu insisted that he could be as human
and as fun loving as any other man. Anne bade him
prove it by dressing as a circus clown and dancing a
saraband for her. She said she would hide behind
the curtains of a room in the palace and watch him
do it. Then, were she convinced that he could really
unbend and could she overcome her fear of his lofty
dignity, she would come forth and tell him so.

The all-powerful Richelieu—the man of blood,
whom even the haughtiest nobles feared—so far lost
every remnant of sanity as to do as the queen bade
him. As a harlequin, he capered and leaped about
the empty room, his eyes ever on the curtain at its
far end.

Suddenly, in the midst of his idiotic performance,
the curtain was dashed aside; a howl of laughter swept
the room; and the queen stood revealed to his gaze.
Clustered around her and reeling with mirth were a
score of courtiers; men and women both.

From that day Richelieu was Anne's sworn foe.
He wrecked her repute with the king, and for a long
time managed to have her kept a prisoner in the palace. In a thousand ways he made her life a torment.

And now, through the grim cardinal's love for

Ninon de L'Enclos, Anne thought she saw a way of striking back at her enemy. She sent for Ninon, chided her for her mode of living, and ended by ordering her sharply to retire at once to a convent. Ninon simply smiled at the command, curtsied to the queen, and said demurely:

"I will gladly go to any convent your majesty may designate—just as soon as I become as unattractive to men as is the woman who wants to send me there."

She left the royal presence. And so great was the power of the girl's beauty in the hearts of those in France's high places, Anne did not dare put her command into effect. The tale of the conversation spread like the prehistorically bromidic "wildfire," and Ninon won new laurels thereby.

The Duke of St. Evremond, at that time one of the greatest men in Europe, offered her his heart and his princely fortune. She replied that his heart was a precious gift which she would prize forever—or for a month or two at the very least; but that she had no use whatever for his fortune, as she had all the money she needed and more would be only a burden.

And the duke—veteran of many a love affair where fortunes had counted for far more than hearts—made the quaint, historic reply:

"Mademoiselle, tu es un honnete homme!" (Mademoiselle, you are an honest man!")

Three generations of Sevignes—father, son, and grandson—in turn loved Ninon during her seventy-five years of heartbreaking. Love for her seemed a hereditary trait in the Sevigne family.

But it was the old Duke of St. Evremond, of all her numberless wooers, for whom Ninon cared most. Though their love was soon dead, they remained loyal and devoted friends to the day of the duke's death. Their correspondence—prettily formal, yet with an undercurrent of true affection—is still extant. And through life Ninon ran always to the duke with every sorrow or perplexity; notably when, at the age of sixty, she discovered her first wrinkle, an all but invisible crease between her brows. In horror she related to St. Evremond the fearful tragedy. With a laugh he banished her dread.

"That is no wrinkle, **ma petite**," he reassured her. "Love placed it there to nestle in."

The mighty Prince de Conde, the left-handedly royal D'Estrees, La Rochefoucauld (the Machiavelli of France,) and many another of like rank and attainment were proud to count themselves Ninon's worshipers. To no one did she show more favor than to another. King of France or Scarron, the humpback poet—so long as they could amuse her, Ninon gave no thought to their titles or wealth or name. To her, one was as good as another. To none did she give fidelity. Nearly all of them she treated outrageously. Yet of them all, only one was ever driven away by her caprices before she was fully ready to dismiss him.

That sole exception was the gallant Comte de

Fiesque, who, for a brief space of time, held her wandering heart and thoughts.   Ninon as a rule was not
quarrelsome.   But she and De Fiesque were as flint
and steel.   Their affair was one fierce series of spats
and disputes that blazed out at last in a pyrotechnic
row.

As a result of this climax quarrel, De Fiesque scuttled away in red wrath, vowing that he was forever
and ever done with so ill-tempered and cranky a
woman as Ninon de L'Enclos.

Ninon was aghast.   Paris was aghast.   France was
aghast.   The love world at large was aghast.   For
the first time in her whole hectic life, Ninon de L'Enclos had been deserted—actually **deserted!**   And by
a nobody like De Fiesque!   She who had snubbed a
king, had tired of Condez, had yawned daintily in the
half-monarchical face of D'Estrees himself!

It was unbelievable.   For an instant her fame as
a peerless and all-conquering Wonder Woman threatened to go into partial eclipse.   But only for an instant.

De Fiesque, placed during a little hour on a pinnacle
of flaring originality, began to receive tenderly re-
proachful letters from Ninon, beseeching him to come
back to her, saying she had been wrong in their dis-
pute, begging his forgiveness—Ninon, to whom
princes had knelt trembling!—promising all sorts of
meek, womanly behavior if only he would cure her
heartbreak by a word of love.

These letters of hers to her deserter would have moved an equestrian statute to maudlin tears. But De Fiesque's pride had been too deeply cut by that last quarrel, to let him relent. Besides, he was vastly enjoying his novel position as the only man on earth to whom Ninon de L'Enclos had made such an appeal. So while his fellow courtiers alternately envied him and longed to kick him, they wondered what might be the secret of his fascination over Ninon.

Thus, for a few days, matters stood. Then Ninon hit on a master stroke. The thing that had first attracted De Fiesque to her had been the glory of her red-gold hair. He had loved to bury his face in its shimmering, soft masses, to run its silk strands through his fingers. Incidentally, in the course of their epoch-marking quarrel, he had called Ninon supremely vain and selfish.

Now she cut off all her wonderful hair; cut it off, wrapped it up, and sent it, without a word of explanation, to De Fiesque. He understood. She had made this supreme sacrifice for him—for the man who had deserted her. To him she was offering this chief beauty of hers.

De Fiesque's pride vanished. Through the streets he ran, bareheaded, to Ninon's house. Into her presence he dashed and flung himself at her feet, imploring forgiveness for his brutality and vowing that he loved her alone in all the world.

But the rest of the dialogue did not at all work out

along any recognized lines of lovers' reconciliations. Ninon patiently heard to an end De Fiesque's blubbered protestations of devotion. Then, very calmly and triumphantly, she pointed to the door.

The interview was over. So was the affair. Ninon de L'Enclos was vindicated. No lover had ever permanently deserted her. There was no man so stubborn that she could not lure him back to her. The De Fiesque incident was closed. All that remained for Ninon to do was to introduce among Paris women a temporary fashion of wearing the hair short. Which she promptly did. And thus she suffered not at all by her ruse.

Some two centuries later, George Sand, who had read of the incident, tried the same trick to win back Alfred de Musset. In her case, it was a right dismal failure. De Musset, too, was entirely cognizant of the story of Ninon's shorn hair. And even without her hair, Ninon was lovely; while, even with hers, George Sand was hideous.

Queen Christina of Sweden came to France. Ninon delighted the eccentric Swede. Christina made a confidante and familiar friend of her. She begged Ninon to return with her to Sweden, promising her a title and estates and a high place at court.

Ninon called unexpectedly at Christina's Paris apartments one morning to talk over the plan. She entered the queen's drawing-room unannounced. There on the floor lay a man, one of the Swedish officials in Christina's suite. He was dead—murdered —and was lying as he had fallen when he had been stricken down.

Above him stood Christina, at her side the assassin who had struck the blow. The queen turned to Ninon and explained. The official had displeased her majesty by some undiplomatic act; and taking justice into her own hands, Christina had ordered another member of her suite to murder the offender. She was as unconcerned over the killing as if she had ordered a rabid dog to be shot.

Ninon fled in panic fear from the apartment. Nor ever again could she be induced to come into the presence of the royal murderess. Thus ended the Swedish project.

Though the confidential friendship of one queen was thus taken forcibly from Ninon, she had later the satisfaction of helping on the cause of another and uncrowned queen. It is her one recorded experience in dabbling with politics, and the role she played therein is interesting.

King Louis XIV.—son of that Anne of Austria who had hated Ninon—had reached the age when life began at times to drag. The "Grand Monarque" had still fewer reasons than those of Ninon's father to deplore the missing of any good times. But youth had fled from him at last. He found himself, in middle age, a sour-faced, undersized man, with a huge periwig, a huger outjutting beak of a nose, and wearing egregiously high boot heels to eke out his height. People—a very few of them and at a safe distance— were beginning to laugh at his pretensions as a lady-killer. Nature, too, was proving herself less a tender mother than a Gorgonlike stepmother, by racking him with dyspepsia, bad nerves, and gout.

These causes led him to turn temporarily to what he termed "the higher life." In other words, by his whim, the court took to wearing somber garments, changing its scandalous conversation for pious reflections and its unprintable novels for works on philosophy. Whereat, yawns of boredom assailed high Heaven.

In the course of his brief penitence, Louis frowned majestically upon his tempest-tempered favorite, Madame de Montespan. And she—tactless or over-sure of her position—scowled back, harshly derided the new order of affairs, and waxed more evil-tempered than ever.

In Madame de Montespan's household was a certain Madame de Maintenon, widow of the hump-backed little Scarron, who had once sued for Ninon de L'Enclos' favor. Strangely enough, his widow and Ninon were close friends. And at this court crisis, Ninon made the term "friendship" mean something.

She herself had plainly shown that she had no interest in the king. Now she set to work to make the king feel an interest in Madame de Maintenon, whom Louis in his long period of gayety had always disliked. Ninon taught the widow how and when to throw herself in the king's way, and how to treat him. She coached her friend as a stage director coaches a promising but raw actor.

As a result, when Louis came, smarting, from a squabble with the fiery De Montespan, he would find himself, by the merest chance, in the presence of De Maintenon, whose grave gentleness and attitude of awed devotion served as balm to his quarrel-jarred nerves.

He took to seeking out the wise and gentle widow —of his own accord, as he thought—and spending more and more time in her company. And De Maintenon, carefully coached by Ninon, the queen of heart students, managed to awaken in the deadened royal brain a flicker of admiration that slowly warmed into love.

At that point Ninon's genius achieved its most brilliant stroke. Under her instructions the widow gave the king's advances just the right sort of treatment. She made it clear to Louis that she scorned to be a royal favorite.

As a result, one midnight, there was a secret wedding in the palace chapel; King Louis XIV. becoming the legal, if unacknowledged, husband of the penniless humpback's meek widow; Ninon, it is said, being one of the ceremony's few witnesses.

Ninon had "played politics" just once—and with far-reaching results to history; as De Maintenon's future influence over her husband was to prove. Among the results, the revocation of the Edict of Nantes is laid at De Maintenon's door, an act that partly depopulated France and partly populated America.

By this time Ninon had become something more than a winner of hearts and a setter of fashions. She found herself a social arbiter as well. Without an introduction to the illustrious Ninon de l'Enclos and a word of indorsement from her, no young man could hope to make his way in Paris society. Noblemen in the country, sending their sons to Paris for a career, moved heaven and earth to obtain for them letters of introduction to Ninon.

Her lightest expression of opinion was everywhere quoted as inspired. With a smile or a frown she could make or unmake men's futures at court. Had she so chosen, she might have become, with this amazing amount of power, a most unbearable tyrant. Instead, she used her power wisely and kindly. Charitable to a fault, her tact and her money and her boundless influence were always making the way easy for some one or other.

For instance, in her old age—or rather in what would have passed for old age in any other woman—she took an interest in a wizened, monkeylike boy of the people. She set him on the path to advancement and supplied him with the money for his education. To his dying day, the little man remembered her with a veneration most people would have bestowed on a saint; even though he used the education she had given him to help in tearing down the monarchy whose nobles had been his benefactress' slaves. He is known to fame as Voltaire.

Years came and went. They merged into decades and quarter centuries. The men who once had loved Ninon de L'Enclos grew old and died, and their places were taken by sons and then by grandsons. Dynasties changed. The world rolled on. New times brought new customs.

But Ninon remained unchanged. Still beautiful, still vibrant with all her early gay charm, she remained to outward appearances what she had been for the past fifty years. The grandsons of her girlhood suitors were as madly in love with her as had been their grandsires. In love, in society, in fashion, she was still the unquestioned sovereign.

Throughout Europe, there was now no one who doubted the unadorned truth of the story concerning the Man in Black; for it seemed that no mortal agency could have kept any woman so perennially young. As the years passed, folk fell to speculating on how many drops of the precious rose-colored liquid might still remain in the phial. And, in scared voices, they repeated the prophecy of the man in black:

"You shall see me once again three days before your death."

Perhaps, now that you know Ninon better, you may

laugh less contemptuously at the tale of the Man in Black; or, at the least, credit her with believing it. Throughout her life, she never changed the story in any way; nor could the shrewdest cross-examining lead her to contradict herself about any of its most minute details. A haunting fear of the Man in Black's promised return was always in her mind, even during her gayest days and nights.

As late as her ninetieth year men made vehement love to her. At an age when most women are withered crones, she still broke hearts. Men fought duels by the dozen for her favor. In her old age a youth blew out his brains on her account.

During her later years a great sorrow came to her. Through no conscious fault of her own, she was enmeshed in what was probably the most horrible tragedy of its sort in history. This tragedy cannot even be touched on here. In no book written in the English language can you find its complete details. It is enough to say that the nameless horror of it wrecked Ninon's health and her mind, leaving her for the time a mental and physical wreck.

Slowly she recovered her health, her brain, and her unquenchable spirits. Her beauty had never been impaired. And once more she ruled as queen of hearts. Now, too, she blossomed forth into literature, becoming with ease a famous author. Her essays were quoted, imitated, lauded to the skies.

Nor is there the slightest reason to doubt that she

was their author. Always bluntly honest to a fault, the woman who would not accept rank or money was not likely to accept the literary ideas of others and pass them off as her own. Also, the style of her published work was identical with her private letters.

It is odd, and possibly—or possibly not—significant, that of the world's superwomen, more have leaned toward literature than toward any other one pursuit. The gift of writing comes nearer to being their one common trait than do beauty and all the other hackneyed siren charms. The power that enables such women to win hearts appears to manifest itself by use of the pen.

To instance a very few of the hundreds of heartbreakers who were also authors, letter writers, and so forth, of greater or less note, one has but to recall George Sand, Adah Menken, Adrienne Lecouvreur, Ninon de L'Enclos, Lola Montez, Madame de Sevigne, Madame Recamier, Madame Roland, and Marie Stuart.

By 1706 there was scarce a man or woman left alive who remembered Ninon when, as a girl, she had come first to Paris. Youths who had worshiped her as a middle-aged woman were now aged men. She herself was ninety.

To say that she was still a girl in looks and actions is a gross exaggeration, of course; not the firmest believers in the Man in Black claimed that. But, at ninety, she was still beautiful, still alluring and adorable, as men continued to learn. Younger women—

women young enough to be her grandchildren—were neglected for her sake. It is said that on her ninetieth birthday she received a fervent declaration of love from a noble who had met her but a few days earlier.

Then came the end. On one day, in 1706, Ninon de L'Enclos was in blooming health; on the next she was dying. She wrote a single line to one of her friends and dispatched it by a messenger.

The letter did not find the woman to whom it was addressed until nearly a week later. Three days from the time she wrote it, Ninon died. The friend, opening the letter, read, scrawled in a fear-shaken hand, this sentence:

"I have just seen the man in black again!"

CHAPTER THREE

PEG WOFFINGTON

IRISH HEART CONJURER

A THRONG of people—barefoot peasants, modish idlers, tradesfolk, riffraff—stood in a Dublin courtyard one day in 1727, providing the much-admired "sea of upturned faces." All eyes were raised, all necks were back bent. Every one was looking aloft to where a taut wire was stretched between two post tops.

Along the wire walked a harlequin, taking mincing dance steps and balancing across his shoulders a pole from whose extremities dangled two huge baskets. To make the feat the more interesting by adding a spice of possible peril, announcement had been made that each basket contained a live child.

The chance of a triple tragedy in the event of a misstep made the tight-wire walk a right diverting spectacle, and thrilling withal, to the good folk of Dublin. But half way between the two extremity posts, still a new element of interest was added.

For, at that point, the top suddenly popped off one of the baskets, and a big-eyed, laughing face beamed down, over the edge, at the crowd.   The face of a seven-year-old child—a girl.   A roar of applause followed upon the youngster's unrehearsed appearance.

Thus did Peg Woffington, a queen of her century's actresses and consummate heart conjurer, make her professional debut.

Peg—her full first name, which nobody dreamed of using, was Margaret—was the daughter of an Irish bricklayer who had one point in common with certain modernists in that he was rabidly opposed to all doctors.

And the medical guild had in due time its revenge on the sacrilegious brick artist.   For once, when Woffington fell ill, he fiercely refused to have a physician summoned.   And he rapidly grew better.   As her husband was convalescing, Mrs. Woffington sought to make assurance doubly certain by calling in a doctor.   The pill juggler looked at the invalid and pronounced him out of danger.   Next day Woffington died.

Peg was just learning to walk at the time of her lamented father's tilt with the cult of Æsculapius.   She and her baby sister, Mary, at once set about helping to earn their own living, by toddling on either side of their mother when the widow hawked watercress through the streets, and shrilly piping in duet the virtues of her wares.

To Dublin, when Peg was seven, came one Madame Violante, with a troupe of tumblers and rope dancers. Peg was apprenticed to Madame Violante. But her term of service as a baby acrobat was short. Her employer had better use for her.

It was Madame Violante who originated the ever-since-popular custom of producing famous plays and operas, with child actors filling all the roles. Her "Lilliputian Troupe" scored a big success in Dublin and the provinces. Much of this success was due to Peg, who almost invariably was cast for old-woman parts, and who "doubled in the brass" by doing quaint little step dances between the acts.

It was cruelly hard work for a growing child; nor was the early eighteenth-century theater the very best sort of nursery and moral training school for little girls. But apart from other and less creditable lessons acquired, she learned stage presence and practically every art and trick of the profession.

From the "Lilliputian Troupe," Peg graduated into the more lucrative and equally moral pursuit of theater orange vender. In slack seasons, when no cargo of oranges chanced to have landed recently from the Americas, she acted, off and on; playing, at twelve, mature roles in provincial theater comedies, and exhibiting a rollicking humor that carried her audiences by assaut. At seventeen, she was playing—at seven dollars and fifty cents a week—Ophelia and other exacting parts.

Incidentally, on both sides of the footlight candl
as actress and as orange girl in the pit——she had
since made herself the toast of the Dublin beaux.
was pretty—though not strikingly so.   She ha
ready, and occasionally flaying, Irish wit.   She
too, the magic, if still undeveloped, fascination oi
super-woman.   As to her morals—they were
morals of any and every other girl of her environi
and upbringing.   She was quite as good as she k
how to be.   There was not a grain of real vice in
whole cosmos.

But there was a blazing ambition; an ambition
was cramped and choked in the miserable, make
provincial playhouses.   She burned to be a far
actress.   There was no chance for her in Ireland.
she came to London.

It was a case of burning her bridges behind
For she carried a worn purse that held seven
shillings.   And the not-overnew dress she wore
her sole wardrobe.   These were her tangible as
On this capital and on genius and pluck and amb
and good looks and the charm that was daily gro'
more and more irresistible, Peg relied to keep
going.

To manager after manager she trudged.   Not
would find work for her.   In all, she made nine
applications.   And she scored just precisely nine
rank failures.

Finally, half starved and wholly discouraged,

succeeded in interesting the manager of the Covent
Garden Theater. And he gave her, or sold her, the
chance she sought—the chance to appear before a
London audience.

Her first appearance on the metropolitan stage was
all that was needed to prove her worth. At once she
caught the public fancy. Soon she found herself the
most popular actress in England.

An air of mingled sadness and gayety in her stage
work, an audacity and fresh youthfulness—and the
mystic charm—carried her straight to the front. At
this period she touched nothing but comedy—at which
she had no peer—and preferably played male roles.
Masculine attire set forth her stunning figure, and she
played devil-may-care, boyish parts as could no other
woman.

One night, after the first act of "The Constant
Couple," wherein, clad in small-clothes and hose, she
was playing **Sir Harry Wildair,** Peg ran laughing and
triumphant into the greenroom. There she chanced
to find her bitterest friend and rival, Mistress Kitty
Clive, a clever but somewhat homely actress. Said
Peg in delight:

"They applauded me to the echoes! Faith, I believe half the men in the house thought I was really
a boy."

"Perhaps," sneered envious Kitty. "But it is
certain that at least half of them knew you
weren't."

Peg stopped short in her gay laugh and eyed Kitty's plain visage quizzically.

"Mistress Clive," observed Peg, in irrelevant reflection, "did you ever stop to consider how much utterly useless modesty an ugly woman is responsible for unloading upon this poor world of ours?"

Kitty did not again cross swords with Peg. Indeed, after the first encounter, few people did.

The fops, the wits, the macaronis, the bloods, the Corinthians—all had discovered Peg long before this time. She was their darling, their idol. As this poor article is too brief in scope to contain a transcript of London's Social and Club Register of the day, most of Peg's minor conquests must be passed over without a word. One or two alone stand out as worth a few sentences.

Macklin, matinee favorite and really great actor, fell heels over head in love with her. So did Hallam, the doctor-author. Macklin, having no hope of winning Peg's favor, was content to watch over her and to guard her like a faithful bulldog. Hallam was not so humble.

Peg did not inherit her father's hatred for doctors, for she flirted lazily with Hallam and amused herself with his admiration. In time she tired of him and frankly told him so.

Hallam, lacking the game, sought the name. Furious at his dismissal, he was still eager to be considered a successful wooer of the famous actress. So he took to boasting loudly at White's and the Cocoa Tree that Peg cared for him alone, and that she had written him reams of burningly ardent love letters.

Peg heard of the boast and was foolish enough to run to the devoted Macklin with the story, entreating him to punish the braggart.

Macklin did not wait to write a challenge, or even go home for his sword, which he did not happen to be wearing that day. Snatching up his cane, he rushed to a near-by coffeehouse where he knew Hallam was likely to be found at that hour. There he discovered the author-doctor drinking with a circle of friends, to whom he was descanting upon Peg's worship of himself.

Macklin sprang at Hallam, seized him by the throat, and caned him unmercifully. Hallam writhed free and whipped out his sword. Macklin, forgetting that he himself was wielding a cane and not a sword, parried Hallam's first thrust and lunged for the doctor's face.

The ferrule of the cane pierced Hallam's left eyeball and penetrated to his brain, killing him instantly—an odd climax to one of history's oddest duels.

Macklin was placed on trial for his life. But he was promptly acquitted. And Peg's renown glowed afresh, because, through her, a man had died.

A pamphlet, written by still another vehement admirer, contains a description of Peg Woffington, written about the time of Hallam's taking off. Part of this word picture is worth repeating verbatim. You will note that, though contemporary, it is in the past tense. Here it is:

> Her eyes were black as jet, and, while they beamed with ineffable luster, at the same time revealed all the sentiments of fair possessor. Her eyebrows were full and arched, and had a peculiar property of inspiring love or striking terror. Her cheeks were vermilioned with nature's best rouge, and outvied all the labored works of art.
>
> Her nose was somewhat of the aquiline, and gave her a look full of majesty and dignity. Her lips were of the color of coral and the softness of down and her mouth displayed such beauties as would thaw the very bosom of an anchorite. Her teeth were white and even. Her hair was of a bright auburn color. Her whole form was beauteous to excess.

In the heyday of her glory, Peg went "to drink a dish of tea" with a party of friends one afternoon. Among the guests was a slender little commercial man, a wine merchant, in fact; shrewd, stingy, and smug. How such a character as his could have awakened the very faintest response in impulsive, big-hearted Peg's is one of the innumerable mysteries of hearts.

But at first glance she loved the little man; loved him as never before she had loved, and as she would never love again. She had met the love of her life.

She asked to have him introduced. The little vintner, tickled that the great Mistress Woffington should

have deigned to notice an unknown nonentity, was
duly brought up and presented.

Peg, her head swimming, did not at once catch his
name and bade him repeat it. Obediently, the dapper
youth replied:

"David Garrick, madam."

In the hour that ensued, Peg led Garrick to talk
about himself—a never-difficult task. He told her
that he hated his trade and that he was not making
money thereby. Peg, appraising the man's appearance
as well as a woman newly in love could hope to, saw
that, though short, he was graceful and strikingly
handsome. Also, that he had a marvelous voice.

Abruptly, she broke in on his soliloquy by suggest-
ing that he go on the stage. Garrick stared. She
spoke of the glories of a star's life. Garrick yawned.
She mentioned that successful actors drew large sal-
aries. Garrick sat up and began to listen. When
she went on to speak of the fabulous receipts that
awaited a star, Garrick feverishly consented to her
plan.

Peg set to work, using to the straining point all her
boundless theatrical influence. She got Garrick a
chance. She coached him in the rudiments of acting.
She found that the little wine seller had a Heaven-sent
gift for the stage. So did the managers. So, in short
order, did the public.

Garrick's success was as instantaneous as had been
Peg's own. Peg rejoiced unspeakably in his triumph.

So did he. The lofty motives that actuated Garrick's stage work may be guessed at from this entry in his dairy, October 20, 1741:

> Last night played **Richard the Third** to the surprise of all. I shall make nearly three hundred pounds a year as an actor, and that is what I really dote on.

But he made infinitely more than the prophesied one thousand, five hundred dollars a year. For he speedily became an actor manager. His business training and his notorious stinginess were splendid assets. Money flowed in, beyond his wildest dreams of avarice. And he held on to it all.

Peg was inordinately proud of his achievements. So was Garrick. Peg loved him to distraction. He graciously consented to be loved. Indeed, it is probable that he cared for Peg as much as he could care for anybody except David Garrick. A swarm of women fell in love with him when he made his stage success. In spite of this, he still loved Peg. Even if not exclusively.

Then Peg and Garrick appeared for the time as co-stars. And, with him, she returned to the scene of her early struggles at Dublin. At the Smock Alley Theater there, the two acted in repertoire.

The pair were an enormous hit. So much so that they were forced, by popular clamor, to play straight through the summer. It was one of the hottest summers on record, but great crowds jammed the theater at each performance. An epidemic swept Dublin. A good many of the playgoers caught the infection at the playhouse and died; which caused the epidemic to receive the sinister nickname, "the Garrick fever."

Peg was no less popular than was her colleague. Together they toured Ireland, then came back to London, as openly avowed lovers. They were engaged to be married; but the marriage was from time to time postponed. Always at Garrick's suggestion.

Sir Charles Hanbury Williams, a suitor for Peg's favor at this time, was the author—among half a bookful of odes, sonnets, and so forth, to her charms —of "Lovely Peggy," a popular song "hit" of the day, a stanza of which runs:

> Once more I'll tune the vocal shell,
> To hills and dales my passion tell,
> A flame which time can never quell,
>   That burns for lovely Peggy.
> Ye greater bards the lyre should hit,
> To say what subject is more fit,
> Than to record the sparkling wit
>   And bloom of lovely Peggy.

But Sir Charles wooed her in vain. She had thoughts for no one else but Garrick. One day, reproached by the poet with her greater regard for his rival, and not wishing to cause needless pain to the loser, Peg sought

to evade the charge by saying that she had not seen
Garrick for an age.

"Nay," contradicted the luckless Sir Charles, "I
know you saw him only yesterday."

"Well," she retorted, "and is not that an age?"

She and Garrick had a singular rule for maintaining
their antemarital establishment. It was arranged—by
Garrick—that each should bear the monthly expenses
alternately. When it was Peg's turn, it was noticeable
that much better food was provided and that many
more dinner guests were invited to the house than
during the alternate months when Garrick was running the place.

Once, during a Garrick month, a crowd of people
dropped in unexpectedly to tea. Garrick eyed them
with scarce-disguised hostility. Peg was delighted to see
them. But no more so than if their call had come on her
month for paying the bills, for she was lavishly hospitable, and was always generous—even prodigal to
a fault; traits that caused her thrifty lover much
pain.

Today, as usual, Peg brewed the tea. Glancing at
his own new-filled cup, as Macbeth might have glared
at the imaginary Banquo, Garrick groaned aloud:

"Peg, you've made this tea so strong it's as red as
blood. Zounds, ma'am, d'ye think 'tis to be bought
at a penny the pound that you squander it so?"

It has ever been the fashion of romantic chroniclers,
in writing of this strange union, to paint Peg as a

suffering saint and Garrick as a crank. The latter picture is flawless. The former, unluckily, is not.

For, though Peg loved the actor manager and—
temporarily—loved no one else, yet it was not in her
superwoman nature to rest meekly content with the
attentions of one man. Even though that man chanced
to be the celebrated Davy Garrick. Running through
the warp of her love was a woof of flirtations.

For one instance, Lord Darnley, a rich and notorious
Piccadilly gallant, proclaimed himself her adorer. Flat-
tered at so famous a nobleman's love, Peg flirted outrageously with Darnley. She even denied to him that
she cared for Garrick.

Once Darnley found Garrick's wig in Peg's boudoir
and railed at her infidelity to himself. Peg explained
that she had borrowed the actor's wig and had brought
it home in order to practice in it a masculine role she
was soon to play at the Drury Lane.

Garrick, in jealous wrath, protested against her affair
with Darnley. So she swore to Garrick that she had
dismissed his rival—and gayly continued to meet
Darnley on the sly. In time, Garrick found her out
and the discovery led to their separation. Afterward,
in remorse, Peg is said to have dropped Darnley. But
then, as usual, it was too late for her renunciation to
do any good except to punish herself.

Time after time Garrick had set back the date of
the wedding. When at last the Darnley crisis came,
Peg asked him frankly if he meant to keep his pledge

or not. He replied gloomily that he did. And he went out and bought a wedding ring. He sighed in utter misery as he slipped the gold loop on her finger. Out flashed Peg's Irish temper.

"If you had ten times the wealth and repute and ability that the world credits you with," she declared, "I would not become your wife after this silent confession."

Almost at once she repented her rash words of release. But Garrick held her to them. He considered himself freed. And they parted. Peg sent back all Garrick's presents. He refused to return hers—they included a pair of diamond shoe buckles she had given him—on the tender plea that they would serve him as reminders of her.

Peg wrote an angry letter, pointing out very clearly the wide gulf between sentiment and graft, and telling Garrick on exactly which side of that gulf his action in regard to the presents placed him. Garrick retaliated by blackening her name on every occasion. She made no reply to any of his dirty slurs; nor spoke of him save in praise.

Thus ended the great love of Peg's life. But there were a host of minor loves to help take its place. Next came Spanger Berry, a fiery Irish actor who, to revenge Peg's supposed wrongs, did his level best on the stage to crowd Garrick out of several of the latter's favorite roles. He did not wholly succeed in this loverly attempt, but he caused Garrick many an hour of uneasiness, and wounded him severely by causing a drop in the actor manager's box-office receipts.

Then came a succession. To quote a biographer who wrote while Peg's name was yet fresh:

An infatuated swain swore that if she did not return his love, he would hang, drown, or shoot himself; and in order not to be responsible for his suicide, she consented to listen to his sighs. Then there came along a gentleman with money who won her affection. Another next presented and outbid the former. Another offered, and she received him in her train.

A fifth appeared, and was well received. A sixth declared his suit, and his suit was not rejected. In a word, a multitude of love's votaries paid their adorations to the shrine of their fair saint, and their fair saint was not cruel.

Then, according to the same chronicler and another. came into Peg's life "a personage." There is no hint as to his identity. Whether she was true to him or not is debatable. But she soon discovered that he had grown tired of her. It was borne to her ears that he was paying court to an heiress; intending to break with Peg, by degrees, if his suit were successful.

The heiress gave a masked ball in honor of her birthday. Peg gained admittance, in male costume, to the affair, and contrived to become her rival's partner in a minuet.

"When she straightway poured so many and such vile stories anent the gentleman's character into the lady's ears that the latter fainted and the ball broke up in confusion."

But Peg had gained her aim, by hopelessly discrediting with the heiress the recreant lover. The match was broken off. Peg felt herself right cozily revenged.

The next wooer was a "person." Not a "personage." He was Owen McSwinney, a buffoon. He was the premier clown of his day and a local celebrity.

McSwinny was fairly well to do. And, when he died soon afterward, it was found that he had left his whole estate—some two hundred pounds a year— to Peg.

It was not long after this that Richard Brinsley Sheridan, in his early prime, engaged Peg at four hundred pounds a season, to play at his theater. Sheridan was fervid in his admiration of the Irish beauty. Perhaps this fact, as well as the marked success she scored in his plays. led "The Rivals' " author to double her salary after the first season.

Yearly she grew more popular with her audiences. Having won a matchless reputation as a comedian, she turned for a time to tragic characters, and won thereby a wholly new renown as one of England's foremost tragedians. But comedy was her forte. And to it she returned.

Peg always vowed she hated the society of her own sex; a lucky thing for her, since she was not received by ladies of quality, as were many of her fellow actresses, and since her sharp tongue and the fact that men went wild over her made her hated by these fellow actresses. But her popularity with men endured, and

she wasted few tears over women's dislikes. Few
superwomen have been popular with their own sex.

Peg was elected president of the famed Beefsteak
Club, and she always presided at the board in man's
attire.

All this time she had been supporting her mother
in a luxury undreamed of in the days of the medi-
cophobic bricklayer. And she had educated and
jealously safeguarded her younger sister, Mary.

Mary became engaged to Captain George Cholmondeley, son of the Earl of Cholmondeley; a glittering
match for a bricklayer's daughter. The earl was justly
indignant and posted away to Peg to break off the
affair, if need be, by bribing her and the entire tribe of
Woffington.

Peg met the irate old fellow with the full battery of
her charm. In a trice she had him bewildered, then
half relenting. Feebly he tried to bluster. Peg cut
him short with:

"My lord, I'm the one to complain; not you. For
now I'll have two beggars, instead of one, to feed."

It was a true forecast, for the earl, despite Peg's
blandishments, withheld for a time his check book.
And in the interim she gave the new-wed pair a house
to live in and the money to run it.

And now for the last "big scene" of Peg's stage
career: For some time she had been ailing. But she
kept on with her acting.

On the evening of May 17, 1757, when she was

at the very acme of her career, she played **Rosalind** at Covent Garden. Throughout the comedy she was at her scintillant best. The house was hers. Wave after wave of frantic applause greeted her, as, still in **Rosalind's** male habiliments, she stepped before the curtain, flushed and smiling, to deliver the epilogue.

Gayly stretching out her arms to pit and stalls, she began the familiar lines. With a gesture of infinite coquetry she continued:

"I would kiss as many of you as had beards that pleased me; complexions that liked me—that liked me———"

She faltered, whitened under her make-up, skipped three full lines, and came to the "tag:"

"———when I make curtsy—bid me—bid me—farewell!"

The last line haltingly spoken, she threw her hands high in air and screamed in a voice of abject terror:

"Oh, God! Oh, **God**!"

It was a prayer, not an oath. Reeling, the actress staggered to the wings, and there fell, swooning, leaving the packed house behind her in an uproar of confusion.

Kindly arms bore her from the stage she was never more to tread. Next day, all London knew that Mistress Peg Woffington had been stricken with paralysis and that from the neck down she was dead. Only the keen-witted brain lived, to realize the wreck of the beautiful body.

Sorrowing crowds blocked the street in front of her house for days, momentarily expecting news of her death. But Peg did not die. She did not die until three tedious years had passed.

Little by little she partly regained the use of her body. But she was feeble. Her rich beauty was wiped out as an acid-soaked sponge might efface a portrait.

Out of the gay life that had been the breath of her nostrils, feeble as an old woman, plain of face and halting of speech—she nevertheless retained enough of the wondrous ancient charm to enslave another adorer.

The newest—and last—wooer was Colonel Cæsar, of the Guards. On learning that Peg in her stricken state had infatuated the gallant colonel, a coffeehouse wit sized up the situation by cruelly quoting:

"Aut Cæsar, aut nullus."

It was a vile thing to say. And Cæsar hunted up the humorist, so runs the story, and thrashed him within an inch of his life.

Some time later, Tate Wilkinson, an "impersonator" of that era—yes, there were pests on the earth, even in those days—was scheduled to give a series of humorous impersonations of famous actors and actresses at the Drury Lane; then managed and partly owned by David Garrick.

Peg feared she might be held up to ridicule by the mimicry. The fear preyed on her mind, to a pathetic extent. Colonel Cæsar went to the theater and there informed Garrick that if he permitted Wilkinson to impersonate Mistress Woffington, the colonel would first give him a public caning and would then call him out.

The impersonation of Peg had been mysteriously lost from the imitator's repertoire when the performance was given.

Peg died in 1760, at the age of forty. She left more than five thousand pounds. She left it to charity. And, as a testimonial to her, a range of low-roofed, wistaria-covered cottages was built for the exclusive use of the poor. The dwellings were known as "The Margaret Woffington Cottages."

Samson's costume would start a panic on modern Broadway, yet it was doubtless deemed correct in his time. Queen Elizabeth's table manners would cause her speedy ejectment from any civilized restaurant, yet she was sixteenth century's model for etiquette. George Washington's spelling would not pass muster in a primary school, though in 1776 he was regarded as a man of high education. While as for Lady Godiva—

New times, new ways. Won't you remember that, in dealing with Peg Woffington? She was a product —and a fine product—of her generation and surroundings. Think of her only as an unfortunate, warm-hearted, beautiful girl, whom men adored almost as much for her lovable qualities as for her siren fascinations.

She merits a pedestal in the temple of superwomen. If I have failed to establish her right to it, the fault is mine, not hers.

CHAPTER FOUR

HELEN OF TROY

MODEL FOR ALL THE SIRENS OF THE CENTURIES

S OME wise folk say she never existed. But, for that matter, some wise folk also say that her press agent, Homer, never existed, and that his "Iliad" and "Odyssey" were compilations of lesser men's writings. As well say that Napoleon was a "compilation" of his marshals.

Some aver that she indeed walked the earth, a Wonder Woman, and that her charm perhaps stirred up strife among nations, but that her fame kept on growing after she was dead, until—even as hundreds of jokes were attributed to Joe Miller that Joe never perpetrated or even heard—people got to making her the heroine of a myriad impossible deeds and adventures that no one woman or no ten women could have achieved.

Still others declare that she and her story were allegorical, standing for feminine charm and for its fatal power; that she embodied the Greek idea of superwoman perfection. The same sort of people gravely tell us that Hercules and Crœsus and William Tell were "solar myths"—whatever that may mean—and their descendants will put the myth brand, ten thousand years hence, on Napoleon, Roosevelt, John L. Sullivan, and Lydia Pinkham.

While common sense may balk at the tale of Helen of Troy, common sense would as readily balk at a narrative of the high cost of living or of the All-Europe War. And what is common sense among friends? I am going to tell Helen's story as if it were gospel truth. For all I know, it may be. I am not going to draw on a dull imagination for any of it, but to take it entirely from a dozen of the olden authorities, from Homer down. After all, since we believe in Santa Claus, why not in Helen of Troy?

(I cannot help feeling a little thrill of pride in this preamble. In spots, it is almost scholarly. And so to the story.)

She was the daughter of Tyndareus of Argos, one of the horde of kinglets who split up the Greek archipelago among them. She lived three thousand years ago. And so adorable was she that some one started a rumor that she was not the daughter of Tyndareus, but of great Jove himself. This kind of talk passed as complimentary in those benighted days. Wherefore, Helen's parents did not start a suit for criminal libel against the flatterer, but heaped honors on him.

By the time Helen reached young womanhood, she

was the wonder of all Greece.   She was tall, slender,
and red-haired.   In a day of almost universal dowdi-
ness, she knew how to wear her clothes—although she
did not use that knowledge to any prodigal extent;
clothes, in balmy prehistoric Greece, being used for
adornment rather than as coverings.

Her wit and her subtle magnetism vied with her
good looks.   Suitors came from one end of the archipelago to the other to visit the palace of Tyndareus
and to pay court to the Wonder Girl.   They were a
goodly throng, these suitors; kings one and all, even
though most of their kingdoms were smaller than Dela-
ware.   Here are a few names culled from the endless
list:

Ulysses, craftiest of Greeks, a short-legged man, with
the upper body of a giant; Agamemnon, overlord of
all Greece, titular King of Mycenæ, a hot-tempered,
long-winded potentate; Menelaus of Sparta, Agamemnon's brother, an honest, not overbright, kind-hearted
chap, who loved sport better than statesmanship; Nestor, the wisest of men, (yet old enough to have known
better than to come a-courting, for already his hair
and beard were white); the two Ajaxes, thickheads
both, one of whom was later to crown a silly life by
defying Jove's lightning to mortal combat; Diomed,
champion heavyweight battler of his century; Achilles,
fiery demigod and prehistoric matinee hero; these and
many another.

Now, in that benighted age, kings had a way of

gratifying personal grudges by declaring war on their fellow sovereigns. Tyndareus was a shrewd old fellow. Also, he was fond of his glorious daughter, and he wanted to save her and her future husband from possible misfortune. So, before he allowed Helen to make her choice he bound each and all of the suitors to the following solemn oath: That they would not only abide peacefully by Helen's decision, but would pledge themselves to fight to the death in behalf of the contest's winner if, at any future time, his domestic peace should be threatened, or his wife stolen from him.

This pledge was not as fanciful as it may seem. For, cave-man tactics of "wooing by capture" were still more or less in vogue. A man who fell in love with another's wife was wont to kidnap her and to defy her bereft spouse to get her back.

Thus, Tyndareus was not only preventing civil war in Greece, but he was making it prohibitively perilous for any outsider to try to win Helen. Such a wooer would find himself at odds with practically every country in the whole archipelago. Yes, decidedly Tyndareus knew what he was about. He was assuring his daughter—as far as was humanly possible—a safe married life.

All the royal suitors—being very much in love—were in a condition to promise anything. They bound themselves, right willingly, to the oath Tyndareus exacted; even Nestor, who, as I think I said, was old

and wise enough to have known better.   It is a supreme
tribute to Helen's glory that the wisest man alive
should have behaved just as foolishly over her as did
the osseous-brained Ajax Telemon.

The oath being taken, Helen's choice was made
known.   And, out of the ruck of greater and richer
and handsomer men, she chose the plodding Menelaus,
King of Sparta.

There were black looks, there were highly unstoical
gusts of anger—but the disappointed suitors made the
best of their bad luck.   After consoling themselves by
getting gloriously drunk at the marriage feast, they
called it a day, and went home; not one of them realizing how fearfully his lovelorn oath was one day to
bind him.   And the golden Helen departed for the
prim little, grim little kingdom of Sparta with her liege
lord, Menelaus.

The years drifted on, lazily, happily, in humdrum
fashion.   If Menelaus were not inspiring as a husband,
he was at least pleasanter to live with than a cleverer
man might have been.   He and Helen had one child,
a daughter, Hermione.

Placid years make sweet living, but poor telling.
So let us get along to the day when heralds from the
port of Pylos brought news of a strange prince's arrival
on the Spartan shores.   The messengers knew not who
the stranger might be, nor whence he came.   But, from
his retinue and dress and bearing, they judged him
worthy to be a guest of honor.   So a gorgeous guard

was sent to escort him to the palace. and great preparations were made there to receive him.

The event seems to warrant a more Homeric wealth
of language than I can compass, but it would be hard
not to drop into semi-stately—not to say semi-Homeric
and wholly plagiaristic—diction over it. So bear with
me. It won't last long.

Adown the dry white road that ran to Pylos through
the plain, a dust cloud was advancing; shields of bronze
and weapons gleaming through it, here and there,
with glimpses of purple robes. In the palace, tables
were set out, with fair linen on them. Meats were
brought forth, with rare wine from the Ismarian vine-
yards to the north. A votive heifer was driven in,
lowing, from the fields, for the guest sacrifice. Her
horns were soon sheathed with gold; then the ax-man
felled and killed her with a single blow. She was
quartered, and her fat was laid on the fire, along with
barley grain And the savor of the sacrifice rose, grateful, to high Olympus.

Now, through the yellow dust cloud, chariots were
to be seen. A hardy band of mariners plodded beside
the wheels and behind. They were bronzed and clear-
eyed, these sea rovers, beguiling the journey with gay
speech and with deep, mighty laughs. And they
shouted. instead of speaking as do landfolk.

In the foremost chariot rode two men. One was
King Diocles of Pherae. The other was the goodliest
man mortal eye ever looked upon. A mane of fine-

spun golden hair fell over the shoulders of his Sidonian robe; his face was like the sunshine, and his eyes were filled with the gladness of living. He was Paris, son of King Priam, and a prince of Troy. And his right hand gripped a shadow-casting spear.

In the banquet hall, when the visitors and their host were seated, appeared Helen, the wife of Menelaus, with her little daughter, Hermoine. When the cries of hunger and of thirst had died down, Helen addressed the strangers, asking no direct question—since to question a guest were discourteous—but saying that mayhap they would deign to explain who they were, and why they had come hither.

Then arose Paris, standing by the board, facing the golden Helen. And he spoke winged words:

It was prophesied at his birth, he began, that he would one day be the ruin of Troy. To prevent his living to fulfill his ordained fate, his father, King Priam —weeping at the deed's black necessity—had him borne to the lonely top of Mount Ida, there to die of exposure, or at the fangs of wild beasts. But a great she-bear, roaming the mountain crest, found the babe and brought him down to her cave, and there laid him among her own soft-coated young. Here he was found one day by herdsmen, among whom he grew up.

In time he owned a herd. The best-loved of his cattle was a white bull, called The Star. Now it came to pass that King Priam, urged on by a dream, sent his slaves to Mount Ida's slopes to secure the finest bull that grazed there, for a sacrifice to Neptune. The slaves came upon The Star and drove him away with them. Paris gave chase, but in vain. Then he hastened to the city of Troy to beg redress from the king. And as he entered the outer gates of Priam's palace, his own sister, Cassandra, recognized him.

Cassandra was a prophetess. Apollo had loved her, and, as a love gift, had endowed her with a gift of foretelling all things. But when she rejected his suit, he willed that while she might still retain the gift of prophecy, her forecasts should never be believed. So now her words were laughed to scorn.

But Priam questioned the mountaineer. And, by the resemblance the youth bore to his father, and the ring that he still wore around his neck, where it had been placed when he had been taken up into the mountain as an infant, the king at last knew him. Great was his joy.

And so, elevated to his rightful princely station, Paris passed the next few years, no longer in the harsh toil and on the poor fare of a herder, but as a king's son; wholly forgetting Œnone, the forest girl of Mount Ida whom he had wooed and won and deserted, and whom he today mentioned merely in the pride of a past conquest.

Now, breaking in upon Paris' somewhat long-winded story of his life, let us come to the real reason of his presence in Sparta. The Goddess of Strife had tried to enliven things in peaceful Olympus by tossing down in front of Venus and Juno and Minerva a golden apple. On the apple's rind was graven the inscription: **"For the most beautiful."**

Straightway, the three goddesses, who had been tolerably good friends, fell to quarreling as to which should have the apple of gold. And they compromised by leaving the decision to Paris. Every member of the trio tried secretly to bribe him; Juno offering him power, Minerva offering him wisdom, Venus promising him love—the love of the fairest woman on earth. Being very young and very human, Paris chose Love; casting aside all hope of power and of wisdom to gain it. And Venus bade him sail forth in search of the Wonder Woman she had promised him. He had departed on this Quest of the Golden Girl, and fate had led him to Helen.

I am not going to touch on the mythological part of Helen's career, more than I can help. But I protest most solemnly that the foregoing tale of Paris and the three goddesses is not mythology, but absolute truth. It may never have happened; indeed, it could not have happened, but it is truth, none the less. If you doubt that a silly apple could cause such strife among three erstwhile friendly deities and stir up unending enmity and discord and hatred, just remember that the apple was of **gold.** Wait until the family estate is divided among the heirs—the heirs who have hitherto been such good friends—and watch what the Golden Apple of Discord can do to breed hate and dissensions.

Those old Greeks were wise, even in their myths. They knew human nature. And human nature's sole change since their day is the substitution of convention. ality for simplicity. At heart, there is no difference.

Take, too, Paris' choice of love, rather than of wisdom or of power. When we read about that, as children, we said smugly: "What a fool Paris was!" Then, as we grew older—Well, if Paris was a fool, just note in what goodly company he stands. His compeers in the same divine idiocy are such immortals as Mark Antony, Marie Stuart, Francis I., almost the whole Bourbon dynasty, Sappho, Cleopatra, Solomon, and a sheaf of other shimmeringly splendid sinners. They were monomaniacs, all of them, and they sold their birthright of decency for a mess of ambrosia; too blinded to know or care how much they were losing, and for how barren a price. Wherein, their particular brand of insanity gives them full right and privilege to claim kinship with the Gadarene swine of Holy Writ.

Well, then, Paris had quested forth to find and win the most beautiful of women. And he found her—at the banquet board of her spouse, Menelaus, King of Sparta.

Long he abode, an honored and trusted guest in his host's palace. And Menelaus suspected nothing, not even that a man of godlike beauty and comfortable dearth of morals was a dangerous visitor in the home of a plodding, middleaged husband.

One night—while Menelaus snored peacefully in preparation for a boar hunt he had planned for the next day—Paris and Helen stole forth together in the darkness and sped, hand in hand, to Pylos, where the lover's ship was in waiting. In his own arms, Paris bore his inamorata from shore to deck. Away across the wine-hued Ægean fled the lovers, to Troy. There they were wed; regardless of the fact that Helen had left a perfectly good husband alive in Greece. The laws against bigamy—if there were any at that day—do not seem to have been very rigidly enforced; nor do those laws' fracturers appear to have lost caste thereby.

Mind you, Helen was no lovesick girl to be swept off her feet by an impetuous wooer with spun-gold hair and a Romeo manner. When Paris stole her from Menelaus and married her, she was forty years old. But, like Ninon de Lenclos and Diane de Poictiers and other of the world's true super-women, age had no power to mar her. Father Time could not pass a face like hers without pausing to kiss it; but the kiss was very tender and loving, and it left in its wake no wrinkles or telltale lines. Helen was ageless.

Ilium worshipped beauty, even as did Greece. And the Trojans, from old Priam down, hailed their new princess with rapture; all save Cassandra, that daughter of Priam who was blest by the gift of prophecy and cursed by the incredulity of all who heard her. At sight of Helen, Cassandra shrieked aloud:

"Trojans, you nurse to your hearts a snake that shall sting you to death! You cherish a firebrand that shall burn our city to the dust!"

And she fell, writhing and foaming, at Helen's feet. But folk laughed at the forecast, and the cheers of welcome drowned the wail of the seeress.

So did Argive Helen come to her husband's people. And thus did her beauty win all hearts. Paris adored her wildly, uncontrollably, to the hour of his death. Her passing infatuation for him soon cooled into contemptuous toleration. And for the second time in her life she learned that a husband is merely what is left of a lover after the nerve has been extracted.

Meantime, Greece was humming like a kicked hornet's nest. Menelaus learned of his wife's flight, and with whom she had fled. He went, heart-broken, to his brother Agamemnon for help in avenging his wrongs. Agamemnon not only reminded him of the other suitors' promise to defend the honor of the man whom Helen should marry, but volunteered, as overlord of Greece, to force them to keep their vows.

Now, this offer was none too easy to carry out. It is one thing to make the maddest pledge, under the drunkenness of love. It is quite another thing to fulfill that pledge when love is dead. The swain who at twenty declares to a girl: "If ever you want me, say the word, and I swear I will come to you, from the ends of the earth!" would be horribly embarrassed if, as a sedate husband and father at forty, that same half-forgotten sweetheart should hold him to his calf-love oath.

So it was with Helen's suitors-emeritus. Long ago they had loved her. She had married some one else. And, during the past twenty years, other interests in their lives had crowded out her memory. If they thought of her at all, it was, now and then, to court domestic tempests by mentally or verbally comparing her golden loveliness and eternal youth with their own wives' dumpy, or slatlike, matronly aspect.

For they had wives, most of them, by this time, wives and children. Just stop for an instant, husbands all, and figure to yourselves what would happen if you should come home tomorrow night and break to your wives the tidings that you were about to go to war— for the sake of another woman! A woman, moreover, whom you had once adored, and whose memory had ever stood, wistful, winsome, wraithlike, between your wives and you.

So, when Agamemnon's fiat went forth that those long-dead promises were to be redeeemed at once, there were home scenes throughout Greece whose bare recital would forever have crushed the spirit of Mormonism. War must have seemed almost a relief to some of those luckless husbands after they had finished listening to their wives' remarks on the subject. For, of all overdue debts in this world of varied indebtedness, the hardest by a million-fold to pay are the sight drafts of defunct sentiment.

These olden heroes were not especially heroic in the crisis that threatened them, and none but a single man will be unduly harsh with them for their reluctance. One after another, they sought to dodge the fulfillment of their pledges.

Ulysses, for example, after an interview with his embarrassingly faithful wife, Penelope—she has always reminded me of Mrs. Micawber—harnessed oxen to a plow and proceeded to give the impression that he had suddenly gone crazy, by plowing furrows in the salt sands of the seashore. Those whose minds had fled were supposed to be directly under divine protection, and naturally such people were never called upon to fight or to meet any other obligation.

Truly, Ulysses was living up to his reputation as the craftiest of the Greeks. Yet his craft was put to naught by the wisdom of old Nestor—one of the few suitors who had not tried to crawl out of his agreement. Nestor placed Ulysses' baby son, Telemachus, on the seashore, in the path of the advancing oxen. Ulysses turned the beasts aside to keep them from trampling the child to death. Whereat, it was decided that Ulysses was not insane—at least, not too insane to do his share of fighting—and he was enrolled as one of the chiefs of the Grecian host.

Having been caught, Ulysses set out, morbidly, to get even with Destiny by catching others. And he, as well as Nestor, began to strip away the subterfuges of the reluctant kings. Achilles, for instance, tried to escape military service by dressing as a girl and hiding among the women of his household. Ulysses, disguised as a peddler, visited these women, carrying a basket full of feminine gewgaws. At the bottom of the basket lay a magnificent sword. While the women were examining the jewelry and clothing in the peddler's stock, Achilles caught sight of the sword. For the first time, he showed interest in the intruder's visit. Paying no heed to the rest of the wares, he picked up the sword and fell to examining it with a professional interest. At once, Ulysses recognized him not only as a man, but as a warrior; and the sulky Achilles was forced to join the expedition.

Day and night, throughout Greece, the smiths' hammers clinked, and the smithy fires roared. Weapons were forged; armor was repaired; army equipments were set to rights. The woods and hilltops reechoed to ax blows, as great trees were felled for ship timber. At last, twelve hundred ships lay at anchor, waiting to bear the avenging host to Troy.

All this preparation was a matter of many months, and for a long time no hint of it reached Troy. Then —first in vague rumor, and soon in form not to be doubted—came news of the Greeks' preparation for war.

By this time, Helen had ceased to be a novelty in Troy. And now men cursed her, beneath their breath, as a sorceress who was to bring war and destruction upon them. Women hated her as the cause of their men's possible death in battle. But Priam, and the noblest blest of his sons—Hector—were still her stanch champions. And, with such backing, her position in the city was at least outwardly assured.

Then came a minor tragedy, a foreshadowing of the wholesale misfortunes that were to follow. I have said that when Paris was still a herdsman on Mount Ida, he had met and loved a forest maid, Œnone, and, on learning that he was a prince, he had promptly deserted her, leaving her to grief and loneliness. Œnone had borne Paris a son—although this was unknown to him. In the years since she had last seen the fickle prince, this son had grown up. He was known as "Corythus." When word reached Œnone of Helen's arrival in Troy, she sent her unfortunate rival a message. She wrote the message on birch bark and dispatched it, by Corythus, to the city.

Corythus arrived at the palace, and was led to Helen's bower, where he begged the princess to dismiss her maids, as he was the bearer of a word for her ears alone. Helen, obeying, received from him the folded birch bark and opened it. She read:

O thou that dost scan these lines, hast thou forgotten quite thine ancient sin, thy palace, thy husband and child—even as Paris hath forgotten me? Thou shalt not forget. For I send thee my curse, with which I shall scourge thee till I die. Soon Paris must look into the eyes of death. And little in that hour will he care for thy sweet lips, thy singing voice, thine arms of ivory, thy gold-red hair. Nay, remembering that thou hast cost his life, he will bid the folk that hate thee have their joy, and give thee to the mountain beasts to tear, or burn thy body on a tower of Troy! My son—and his—beareth this word to thee.

As she finished reading, Helen fell, in a swoon, at Corythus' feet. The youth was alarmed, and dropped on his knees beside her, lifting her head. And at that moment Paris entered the room.

Seeing a stranger kneeling beside Helen, he went wild with jealous rage. Whipping out his sword, he sprang upon Corythus, and buried the blade in the lad's neck. Then he turned, to plunge the weapon into Helen's breast. But, as he turned, he saw the birch-bark message on the floor and stooped to pick it up. Reading it, he realized what he had done, and whom, in his jealous frenzy, he had killed. He flung himself, wailing, forth from the palace and into the night.

Three days later, Corythus was laid on his funeral pyre in the market place of Troy. As Paris was advancing with the lighted torch, Œnone appeared. She leaped upon the pyre and shrieked down at her recreant lover:

"I hear the prayer that thou some day shall make in vain! Thou shalt die, and leave thy love behind thee, for another. And little shall she love thy memory! But"—turning upon the onlookers—"O ye foolish people—see! What death is coming on you from across the waters?"

At the shrieked words, all turned and looked seaward. Bearing down on the coast, in a driving rain, oar blades flashing, sails straining at their rigging, came the long-dreaded Greek fleet.

The Trojan war had begun.

For a highly sporting and poetical and altogether deathless account of that contest, I commend you to Homer's "Iliad." This is the story of Argive Helen, not an uncensored bulletin from the trenches.

For ten years the conflict waged, with varying fortunes. Again and again, as the tide of battle rolled up to the city's very walls, Helen stood on the ramparts and watched her former husband and the other men who had sworn eternal love for her, fighting and dying for her worthless sake.

Once, as she stood thus, she found at her side the group of aged men who were Priam's counselors. Gray-bearded they were, and feeble, and long past the time when love can set the pulse a-flutter, and they hated Helen with a mighty loathing for the disaster she had brought upon their dear fatherland. Even now, they had come forth upon the ramparts to berate her with her sin.

Helen turned and faced them. The afternoon sun poured down upon her white-clad form and upon her wonder face with its crown of ruddy hair. And, at sight of her, these ancient moralists forgot why they had come hither. With one voice, cried they aloud that the love of so glorious a woman were well worth the loss of Troy—aye, of all the world.

A hundred commentators have said that this tribute of the graybeards is the most supreme compliment ever paid to mortal woman's charms.

Paris was at last challenged by Menelaus to mortal combat. He accepted the challenge, but later fled, in terror, from the man he had wronged. Soon afterward, he led a sortie one night against the Greeks. A man on the outskirts of the Grecian camp gave the alarm and let fly an arrow at the advancing Trojans. The shaft struck Paris, inflicting a mortal wound.

The dying man was borne back into the city, and to the palace where the thoroughly disillusioned Helen awaited him. Since his cowardice in fleeing from Menelaus, she had taken no pains to hide her contempt for him. Now, as he lay dying, she looked down without emotion on the sharer of her crime. And Paris, seeing her bend over him, spoke the pitiful farewell that Andrew Lang's verse has made sublime, and that, even in mere prose, cannot lose all its beauty. His voice weak, his eyes glazing, he said:

"Long ago, dear, we were glad—we who never more shall be together. Will you kiss me, once? It is ten weary years since you have smiled on me. But, Helen, say farewell with your old smile!"

Helen, something of her dead tenderness coming back to her, kissed him. And, with her kiss, his life went out.

The torch was set to the unlucky prince's pyre. From the crowd around it sprang Œnone. She mounted the blazing pile of wood, and her body was consumed with that of the man who was not worth dying for.

Helen, almost at once, married Paris' younger brother Deiphobus.

One morning the **Trojans awoke to find** that all the Greeks had sailed away. Their huts stood abandoned on the beach, their ships were nowhere visible on the horizon. Coming back, rejoicing, to the city. the scouting party that brought this joyous news found a monstrous wooden horse. They thought that the Greeks had built it and left it there, to propitiate Neptune for a speedy and safe voyage back to their native shores.

The Trojans bore the horse within the city's walls, to keep it as a memento of the great war.

Helen, passing near the wooden beast that night, heard within it the clank of arms. She halted, and, in a low voice, spoke the names of some of her old suitors. Ulysses answered, bidding her open a concealed trapdoor in the horse's side. She obeyed. Out climbed a score of Greeks. Guided by Helen, they unbarred the city gates to the horde outside who had returned in their vessels. One of the greatest massacres of the ages followed. Babies were butchered as they slept, women were cut down as they ran from their beds, half-wakened men were slaughtered like sheep.

Then the torch was applied, and all Troy was burned to ashes.

Helen was saved from death by Ulysses, who took her to Menelaus and demanded kindly treatment for her, pleading in her behalf that she had at the last betrayed the Trojans by setting free the Greeks within the wooden horse.

There was no need for his mediation. No man could harbor wrath against the golden Helen. Mene laus, at the very first meeting of their eyes, forgave and forgot. He opened his arms and his heart to the woman who had wrecked his life and who had brought to death thousands of gallant men. Back to Greece he bore her; back to Sparta, where he installed her once more as his queen. He had first brought her hither in triumph as a mere slip of a girl, to people who had received her with pride. Now she came to Sparta again, a woman of over fifty, to a populace who cursed and reviled her. Widowed wives and weeping mothers spat at her as she passed them on the way to the palace.

But none of this was as hard to bear as had been Agamemnon's parting words—spoken in her presence —to the Greek army on the shores of Ilium. Though his brother was minded to forgive, Agamemnon was not. And to the assembled host he had shouted:

"O ye who overlong have borne the yoke, behold this woman, the very fountain of your sorrows! For her ye left your dear homes long ago, but now the black

ships rot from stern to prow, and who knows if ye
shall see your own again? Aye, and if homes ye win,
ye yet may find—ye that the winds waft and the waters
bear—that you are quite gone out of mind. Your
fathers. dear and old, died dishonored there; your
children deem ye dead, and will not share their lands
with you; on mainland or on isle, strange men are
wooing now the women you wedded. For love doth
lightly beguile a woman's heart.

"These sorrows hath Helen brought on you. So
fall upon her straightway, that she die, and clothe
her beauty in a cloak of stone!"

The crowd had armed itself with stones as Agamemnon began to speak. But, as he denounced her, they
were looking at her upturned face. And from their
nerveless hands the stones fell to earth. They found
her too beautiful for death.

Agamemnon, looking at her, cried:

"Hath no man, then, avenged his wrongs by slaying
thee? Is there none to shed thy blood for all that
thou hast slain? To wreak on thee the wrongs that
thou hast wrought? Nay, as mine own soul liveth,
there is one. Before a ship takes sail, I will slay thee
with mine own hand!"

But, as he advanced toward her, sword in hand,
her beauty seized him in its spell. He paused, irreso-
lute, then turned away.

For many years thereafter, Helen and Menelaus
dwelt together at Sparta. And because the years

were happy, both history and fable are silent about them, save that Menelaus was once more as slavishly enamored of his wife as in their first months together. Helen, too, was well content with this safe haven after her tempest-tossed decade—"Peace after war; port after stormy seas; rest after toil."

The hatred of the people at large did not much distress her. Through the latticed windows of the palace filtered the growls of the populace, droning and futile as the roar of distant breakers. And even as breakers have no peril for landsmen, so, safe in her husband's home, Helen did not fear the grumbles of the folk he ruled.

Then, in the fullness of his age, Menelaus died, and all at once the situation changed. Helen was no longer safe ashore, listening to the breakers; she was in their power. Her husband's protecting influence gone, she was at the mercy of his subjects; at the mercy of the merciless.

The women of Sparta banded together and, in dangerous silence, advanced upon the palace. These were the mothers, the wives, the daughters, the sweethearts, of men who had left their white bones on the Trojan seacoast, that the golden Helen might again rest snug in the shelter of Menelaus' love. There was not a doubt as to the militants' purpose. And as they drew near the palace, Helen fled. One or two slaves, still faithful to her, smuggled the fugitive out through a rear gateway and through the forests toward the seashore. There, a handful of silver bought a fisher's boat and the service of his crew.

And once more across the "wine-hued Ægean" fared the golden Helen, not this time in girlish light-heartedness to her husband's home, or, in guilty happiness, fleeing from that house by night with the man who had bewitched her, but a fugitive scourged forth from the only home she knew.

Storm-driven, her boat at last was blown ashore on the island of Rhodes. There she found she had been running toward ill fortune just as rapidly as she had thought she was running away from it. The Queen of Rhodes had lost a husband in the Trojan war. And, like every other woman on earth, she had sworn the vengeance oath against Helen. So, the story goes, when the fugitive was brought before the Rhodian queen, the latter gave a single curt order. In obedience to that fierce command, Helen was led forth and hanged; her executioners being blindfolded, that they might not balk at destroying the world's loveliest creation.

So perished the golden Helen. For her sin, she is known to fame as "Helen of Troy," not "Helen of Sparta," or even "Helen of Argos." Posterity has branded her, thus, with the name of the land she destroyed, instead of the land of her birth.

Poets and dreamers of dreams, even in her own century, have said that Helen did not die; that loveliness such as hers could not be destroyed, any more than can the smile of the springtide or the laughter of the sea. They say she escaped the Rhodians and set sail once more upon her wanderings. From shore to shore she voyaged,—ageless, divine, immortal, as eternal as Love itself. Ever, where she went, men adored her and besought her to remain among them to bless or curse their lives. But, ever, women banded together to drive her forth again upon her endless wanderings.

One legend tells of her sojourn in Egypt, and of her meeting, there, Ulysses, "sacker of cities." Penelope was dead, and Ulysses had recommenced his voyaging. He and Helen met, and the old, old love of nearly a half century earlier flared into new flame. And, as ever, Helen's love brought death in its wake. For the Sacker of Cities fell in battle within a few weeks after their reunion.

Another and more popular legend is that Helen, in return for everlasting youth, formed a highly discreditable business partnership with Satan, whereby she was to serve as his lure for the damning of men's souls. Do you recall, in Marlowe's "Doctor Faustus," it was by promise of Helen's love that the devil won Faustus over to his bargain? There is a world of stark adoration in Faustus' greeting cry, as, for the first time, he beholds the enchantress:

"Is this the face that launched a thousand ships
And burned the topless towers of Ilium?
Sweet Helen, make me immortal with a kiss!"

She granted him the kiss, but no immortality; instead, his meed was damnation. like that of her million other swains.

Goethe, in the second part of his "Faust," makes her Marguerite's successor in Faust's love. And one poet after another has amplified the theory that she lives on through the ages, drawing men's souls from them.

And the poets are often right, where sane folk are wrong. The golden Helen—typifying the blind, all-engulfing love that laughs alike at reason and at destruction—lives and shall live while men are men. She lived as Cleopatra, for whom Antony deemed the world well lost. She lives as the hideously coiffured shopgirl with the debutante slouch and the blue-white powdered nose, for whom a ten-dollar-a-week clerk robs the till and goes to jail. And, as in the earliest days of her mortal wanderings, men ever stretch forth their arms to her as she passes, and beseech her to stay her flight long enough to let them damn themselves for her. And, as in those early days, women ever band together in righteous wrath to drive her forth into the darkness.

Poor Helen! Or—is it **happy** Helen? I think the former adjective is to be chosen. For the game she plays can end only in ultimate loss to herself. And that game's true winners, in the long run, are the very women who, fearing her spell over their loved ones, harry her forth to new wanderings. This thought should comfort them in the inevitable hour when golden Helen's shadow shall fall momentarily athwart their placid lives.

The prim path must inevitably triumph over the primrose path.

CHAPTER FIVE

MADAME JUMEL

NEW YORK'S FIRST OFFICIAL HEART BREAKER

FAR to the north, on New York City's westerly side —on One Hundred and Sixtieth Street, near St. Nicholas Avenue—stands almost the sole American memorial to a super-woman. It takes the shape of a colonial dwelling, two and a half stories high, white, crowned by a railed gazebo, and with rear extensions and columns and the rest of the architectural fantasies wherein our new-world ancestors rejoiced.

It is called the Jumel mansion, after Madame Jumel, although it originally belonged to Mary Morris, an earlier and more beautiful man-slayer, at whose dainty feet George Washington, with solemn, but futile, protestations, deposited his heart; and although the woman whose name it bears ended her days there. not as Madame Jumel, but as Mrs. Burr.

The house once stood far in the silent country. But the thin, throbbing island's life crawled northward

inch by inch, until to-day the mansion crouches, mis-
cast and bewildered, amid a forest of new and top-
heavy flat houses—happy hunting ground for none-
too-rich homeseekers—and is shaken by the jar of
"L" and New York Central trains.

Poor old house!   Bewigged and small-clothed
Great-gran'ther Peregrine, from Pompton, caught in
the screaming eddy of a subway rush-hour crowd at
the Grand Central!

So much for rhapsody.   The Jumel place is worth
it.   For there ghosts walk—the stately, lavender-
scented old villains and villainettes who made up New
York's smart set a century and a quarter ago, when
flats were called "rookeries" and polite folk would
scarce mention such things.

In those days, when any theme was too darkly disreputable or indelicate for discussion—and a few
things still were, in that ante-white-slave era—people
were prone to refer to such doubtful topics as
"shrouded in mystery," and to let it go at that.   There
was more than one event in the cradle-to-grave career
of Madame Jumel that called for and received the
kindly mystery shroud.   As far as coherence will allow,
let us leave the shroud snugly tucked around those
events.   I mention it, at the outset, only because more
than one chronicler has used it to account for hiati—(or
is it hiatuses? The former sounds more cultured, somehow—) in the lady's career.   Whereas. nearly all, if
not quite all, these gaps can be bridged quite easily

by well-authenticated facts. Some of them too well authenticated for complete comfort.

And so to the story.

Aboard a ship bound north from the West Indies, one day in 1769, a woman died, a few hours after the birth of her baby daughter. It was not necessary to remove any wedding ring from the dead mother's finger before burying her at sea. One story says that her orphaned daughter's father had been a French sailor named Capet. Another and wholly diverse tale says that the baby was not born at sea at all, but in the Providence, Rhode Island, poorhouse, and of unknown parentage. You see the shroud of mystery was pressed into service very early in the biography.

In any event, soon after the ship touched at Providence, a Rhode Island tradesman's wife was so attracted by the prettiness of the solitary girl baby as to adopt her. At the subsequent christening, the rather uninspiring name of Eliza Bowen was bestowed on the child. No one seems to know why. More mystery, and not a particularly thrilling one at that.

In strait-laced ways and to all demure modesty, Eliza was reared. And at fifteen she was not only the prettiest girl in Rhode Island, but one of the cleverest and—so declared the pious—one of the very worst. In those days and in New England, it was delightfully easy to acquire a reputation for wickedness by merely failing to conform to all the ideas of the blue-law devotees.   Shan't we give Betty Bowen—her commonly used name—the benefit of the doubt?

We know she was not only blessed with unwonted beauty, but with an exceptional mind.   She had, in full measure, even in girlhood, the nameless and irresistible charm of the super-woman.   She was reckless, high of spirit, impatient of restraint; inclined to listen over-kindly, perhaps, to the pleadings of her countless rural admirers.

Then, when she was only seventeen, Colonel Peter Croix came into her life.   Croix was a former officer in the British army and lived in New York.   He had plenty of money, and was more or less what, a century later, would have been called a "rounder."

How this middle-aged Lothario chanced to meet the Rhode Island belle, no one knows.   But meet her he did.   He was the first man of the world who had come into Betty's rustic life.   By contrast with the local swains, he was irresistible.   Or so she found him.   At all events, she did not resist.   She eloped with him, and Rhode Island knew her no more.   Her real career as a heart breaker had set in.

To New York, Colonel Croix brought his inamorata. There he installed her in a stately country house at Thirty-fourth Street and Fifth Avenue, on the spot where, afterward. A. T. Stewart's white marble domicile used to excite the out-of-towners' awe, and where now a trust company's building stands.

Betty wore amazingly costly clothes, paying for a

single dress far more than for her year's wardrobe in Rhode Island. Croix festooned jewelry, Christmas-tree-like, over her neck, hair, and hands. She blossomed like the rose. Croix, inordinately proud of his conquest, also brought shoals of his friends to call, which was a mistake; for Betty had no leanings toward monopolies.

Like the hackneyed, but ever-useful, meteor, Betty flashed upon stark young eighteenth-century New York. The city—so far as its male population was concerned—threw up both hands in blissful surrender.

Croix's friends—some of them rounders like himself, some of them fat, solid, but beauty-loving financiers—formed a court of beauty around the fair newcomer. Betty's consummate charm drew to this court other and loftier men, too.

For example, one of her foremost adorers was a brilliant, magnetic young statesman whose birth was perhaps as unblest as her own, but whose self-made name was already beginning to ring through America. He was Alexander Hamilton. He had a high-born and attractive wife of his own, and an adoring nestful of children. But Hamilton believed in monopolies no more than did Betty, and he became her adorer.

Another of the higher type of men who came a-courting Betty was a statesman of almost equal fame—a little fellow, scarce five feet four inches tall and slight of build, whose strikingly handsome face was lighted by enormous black eyes almost snake-like in their mes-

meric power—particularly over women. He was
Aaron Burr.

Burr was a lady-killer of the first order. He was
not a man of bad morals. He was simply a man of
no morals at all. But he was also a man of no fear.
and a genius withal. He knelt, not in submission, but
in ironic admiration before Betty. And she, like fifty
other women, was swayed by his hypnotic eyes and
his wondrous love eloquence.

At the house of which Croix had made Betty the
chatelaine. Burr and Hamilton often met. but never
at the wish of either. For they hated every bone in
each other's bodies.

They had been at loggerheads as mere lads, when
together they had served on General Washington's
staff during the Revolutionary War. Afterward, in
social and political life, they had clashed, and clashed
fiercely. Now, as rivals for the interest of the volatile
Betty, their smoldering hate flamed forth lurid and
deathless.

And thenceforth. fanned by new political and other
causes, that death hate grew. It came to a head seven
years later, when, in the gray of a chilly morning, the
lifelong rivals faced each other, pistol in hand, in the
fields beyond Weehawken Heights; and when, at the
first volley, Hamilton sprang high in air, then crashed
to the earth, mortally wounded.

Yes. in her time Betty had—directly or indirectly—
much to answer for.

George Washington Bowen, in after years, swore that he was the son of Betty and of the Father of his Country. This the Jumels have fiercely denied.

Among the business-men guests Croix brought to see Betty was an enormously rich old French wine merchant, Stephen Jumel by name. This was in 1804 —the year of Hamilton's death. Jumel was fifty; Betty was thirty-five. Jumel was passing rich; Betty had shrewdness enough to realize that her own fortunes, under her present circumstances, depended solely on her looks and her charm. As beauty is not eternal and as charm sometimes fails to outlive it, the super-woman deemed it wise to accept the infatuated wine merchant's offer of marriage.

Indeed, she is said to have angled with Napoleonic strategy for that same offer, and to have won it only after a sharp struggle of wits. Jumel was no fit opponent for her, then or ever after. From the first, they appear to have had but a single will between them —and that was hers.

On April 17, 1804, Betty and Jumel were married in St. Peter's Church in Barclay Street. The wedding's record still stands in the parish archives. So does the statement made on that occasion by Betty—a statement charmingly at variance with all other records of her origin. For in the church register she wrote that she was born in 1777 and was the daughter of Phœbe and John Bowen—the latter a drowned sea captain.

New York. having a somewhat tenacious memory,

eyed the bride askance—or so she fancied. And, like many a later American, she sought to cover any possible reputation scars by a European veneer. She persuaded her husband to sell out some of his New York interest and to take her to Paris to live. Which, ever obedient, he did.

Napoleon I. was at the heyday of his glory. About him was a court circle that did not look overclosely into peoples' antecedents. Napoleon's brother-in-law, Murat, had started life as a tavern waiter; Napoleon himself was the son of a poor Corsican lawyer and had never been able to learn to speak French without a barbarous accent. As for his sister, Pauline, if "a virtuous woman is a crown to her husband," Pauline's spouse, Prince Borghese, had not a ghost of a chance of skipping into the king row. Nor was Napoleon's first wife, Josephine, of flawless repute. Altogether, it was a coterie unlikely to ask many questions about Betty's early history.

The fascinations of Madame Jumel and the vast wealth of Monsieur Jumel were not to be withstood. Speedily the husband and wife were in the turgid center of things; part and parcel of imperial court life.

As Betty had charmed level-headed New York, there is no need to describe in windy détail what she did to Paris. Her conquests there—like the stars of the Milky Way—shine indistinct and blurred because of their sheer numbers. But through the silvery blur gleams forth the name of Lafayette. The old marquis was delighted, at sight, with the lovely young American; and he eagerly offered to act as her sponsor at court. Which he did, to the amusement of many and to the indefinite advancement of Betty's social hopes.

The great Napoleon glanced in no slightest disfavor on Lafayette's social protegee. He willingly set the seal of imperial approval on the court's verdict The emperor was Stephen Jumel's idol. Himself a self-made man, the old merchant worshiped this self-made demigod, the model and unattainable example of every self-making man since his day.

Jumel's hero-worship took a practical form. He placed his resources at the emperor's service, and once tactlessly, but generously, offered his own wealth and his New York home as solace and refuge in the increasingly probable event of the emperor's mislaying his crown. To which Napoleon replied—speaking, as ever, to the gallery:

"Whatever reverses Fortune may inflict on me, Duty will chain me to France. It would be unworthy my greatness and an insult to my empire for me to seek asylum across the seas."

Yet, when the inevitable Day dawned, the fugitive emperor made plans to do that very thing. And Jumel met him more than halfway by crossing from New York to Havre on his own yacht—the **Elizabeth,** named for his wife—and seeking to bear away his fallen idol to safety. The plan, of course, fell through, and Napoleon in consequence was almost the only Bonaparte who did not sooner or later come to New York.

Imperial friendship and a gloriously extravagant—and extravagantly glorious—wife are things to brag of. They are splendid advertisements. But they are not on the free list. In fact, they rip hideous breaches in the solidest wall of wealth. They played havoc with Papa Jumel's supposedly boundless fortune. One morning in Paris, the Jumels awoke to find themselves nastily close to bankruptcy.

The French court was emphatically no fitting place wherein to go bankrupt. The scared Jumels realized this. Back they scurried to New York; in that bourne of fast-made and faster-lost fortunes to face what the future might bring.

And now, all praise to Betty Jumel, erstwhile queen of money wasters! Instead of repining, or blaming her husband for letting her break him, or flitting to some wooer whose wealth was still intact, she did the very last thing her past would have led any one to expect.

She became, in effect, her husband's business partner. She displayed a genius for finance. It **must** have been stark genius, for her personal experience in the credit side of the money ledger was nil. More through his wife's aid than through his own sound business acumen, Papa Jumel began to win back the ground Betty had so industriously helped him to lose.

One daring and lucky venture followed another. In

an incredibly short time the Jumels were again numbered among the very richest people in America. Once more Betty launched on a career of luxury; but now and ever after she kept just within her abundant resources. Bankruptcy was a peril forever banished.

Betty, you see, did not belong to the type of fool who runs his head twice into the same hornet's nest. There really was no need for such monotony. There were plenty of hornets' nests.

The first expenditure, to celebrate the new fortune, was the buying of the big white house far away on the hillock above the Harlem River; a long, long coach drive, up the Broad Way, from the city's fashionable residence district to the south of Duane Street. Remember, this was a full twenty years before the Southern merchant made his historic speech: "When I come to New York on business, I never think of stopping at the Astor House. It's much too far uptown for a busy man."

The house Betty made her husband buy had been built years earlier by Colonel Roger Morris, after he married Mary Phillipse, the colonial belle, whose father owned most of Westchester County and lived in a manor house there among his vassals like a feudal lord.

To this abode moved the Jumels. Thither they brought a retinue of servants whose numbers amazed the thrifty New Yorkers. Here, too, were deposited such furniture as New York had seldom seen—a marvelously hideous marble-top table given to Papa Jumel by the Sultan of Turkey; a set of chairs that had been Napoleon's; a truly gaudy and cumbrous gold clock, which had been one of the emperor's gifts to Betty; tapestry and pictures that had once belonged to the Empress Josephine; dining-room furniture that had graced the **salle a manger** of King Charles X. of France; a massive, glittering chandelier, the gift of General Moreau, who had vied with the emperor for Betty's smiles.

Above all these and the rest of her home's rich furnishings, Betty treasured two other gifts from Napoleon —odd **gages d'amour** for such a man to have given such a woman. They were the battered army chest and army cot used by him throughout the wonderful Italian campaign that had first established his fame.

The world was scoured by Jumel's merchant ships to secure rare plants and trees for the hundred-and-fifty-acre park surrounding the mansion. Cedars from Mount Lebanon, cypresses from Greece, exotic flowers from South America, roses from Provence—these were but a few of the innumerable exotics that filled the grounds. (The "park," to-day, is a wilderness of dingy, apartment-lined streets).

Once established in their new home, the Jumels began to entertain on a scale that dwarfed even the much-vaunted hospitality of the ante-bellum South. And the people who, of yore, had looked obliquely and frostily on Betty Bowen, now clamored and schemed and besought for invitations to her dinners.

Well they might; for not only America's great folk delighted to honor the mansion by their presence, but every titled foreigner who touched our shores became a guest there.

Hither came Joseph Bonaparte—kicked off the ready-made throne to which his emperor brother had vainly sought to fit the incompetent meager form and more meager intellect—and here he was entertained with royal honor, as if he had been still a sovereign instead of merely a crownless puppet no longer upheld by the mightiest of human hands. Here he was "Your Majesty," and people backed out of the room in which he chanced to be, stood until he gave them gracious leave to sit, and otherwise showered upon him the adoring servility that the freeborn are prone to lavish upon the representatives of monarchy.

Bonaparte after Bonaparte visited the Jumels. The name, "Bonaparte," was still one wherewith to conjure, and that fact by itself made its thick-headed and impecunious bearers welcome in almost every land they might choose to visit. They graciously accepted the Jumel house's hospitality and the veneration of their fellow guests; still more graciously they borrowed money—which they never returned—of Papa Jumel; and most graciously of all they made ardent and heavy love to Betty.

To the Jumel mansion came finally the last and least esteemed of the Bonaparte visitor; a squat, puffy-eyed princeling—pallid, crafty shadow of the Austerlitz Man—who had left France and jail one jump ahead of the police, had served as special constable in London to pick up enough money for food, and now for similar reason was teaching school in Bordentown, New Jersey.

He was Louis Napoleon, alleged nephew of Napoleon I. I say "alleged" on the authority of Victor Hugo's famous sneer that Louis was "neither the nephew of his uncle, the son of his father, nor the father of his son." It was Hugo, too, who, when Louis became emperor of the French, under the title of Napoleon III., dubbed him "Napoleon the Little." For which witticism, Monsieur Hugo was promptly banished from France.

Louis was the son of Napoleon's younger brother of the same name and of his wife—and step-niece—Hortense Beauharnais. The son had not a single Bonapartist feature nor trait. He strongly resembled, however, a certain dashing Dutch admiral, one Flahaut, on whom Hortense had been credited with bestowing a more than neighborly interest. It is not libelous, in view of many proven facts—indeed, it is scarce gossip —to say that Hortense, like her mother, the Empress Josephine, had had the foible of loving not wisely, but too often.

In any event, whoever may have been his father, Louis Napoleon was kindly received by the Jumels: not as a prince, but as a guest of honor. And Papa Jumel lent him much hard-earned American money.

Among all the Bonapartes, Louis was the least promising of the Jumels' beneficiaries. And of them all, he alone was to make any return for their goodness to him.

The Prince de Joinville—here to investigate, and if necessary buy off, Eleazer Williams' claim to be the "lost Dauphin"—stayed at the mansion and paid charming attentions to Betty. So did the polished old scoundrel, Talleyrand, whom Napoleon had daintily described as "a silk stocking filled with muck."

Less lofty of birth, but worth all the Bonapartes put together in point of genius, was a young American poet who vastly admired Betty, and who, on her invitation, spent weeks at a time at the mansion. He was Fitz-Greene Halleck; and, seated on the porch of the Jumel house, he wrote a poem that a million schoolboys were soon to spout—"Marco Bozzaris."

One morning in 1830, Papa Jumel set out for New York on a business call to his bankers. He rode forth from the long, winding driveway—several flat houses and stores and streets cut across that driveway's course today—in the lumbering and costly family coach.

An hour later he was brought home dying. The coach had upset on the frost-rutted road a few miles to the south. Jumel had fallen out—on his head.

Papa Jumel was in the late seventies at the time of his death. His widow was either fifty-three or sixty-one—all depending on whether you believe her own statement or the homely Rhode Island facts. What does it matter? She was one of the super-women who do not grow old.

Scarce was her worthy spouse stretched comfortably in his last sleep, when suitors thronged the house. And it was not alone because the Widow Jumel was one of the richest women in America. She still held her ancient sway over men's hearts; still made sentimental mush of men's brains.

Gossip, silenced of late years, sprang eagerly and happily to life. Once more did New York ring with Betty's daring flirtations. But she cared little for people's talk. She was rich enough, famous enough, clever enough, still beautiful enough to be a law unto herself. The very folk who gossiped so scandalously about her were most eager to catch her eye in public or to secure an invitation to the great mansion on the Harlem.

As to men, she had never yet in all her fifty-three— or was it sixty-one?—years, met her match at heart smashing. But she was to meet him. And soon.

Will you let me go back for a space and sketch, in a mere mouthful of words, the haps and mishaps of one of Betty's earlier admirers?

Aaron Burr was vice president of the United States when he shot Hamilton. The bullet that killed Hamilton rebounded and killed Burr's political future; for Hamilton was a national favorite and Burr was not.

Burr served out his term as vice president amid a whirlwind of national hatred. Then he went West, a bitterly disappointed and vengeful man, and embarked on an incredibly audacious scheme whereby he was to wrench free the great West and Southwest from the rest of the Union and install himself as emperor of that vast region, under the title of "Aaron I."

The scheme failed, and Burr was hauled before the bar of justice on charges of high treason. Through some lucky fate or other, he was acquitted, but he was secretly advised to leave America. He followed the advice. And when he wanted to come back to the United States, he found every port closed against him. So he starved for a time in obscure European lodging.

His heart had been broken, years earlier, by the death of the only woman he ever truly loved. She was not one of the hundreds who made fools of themselves over him. She was not his wife, who had died so long before. She was his only daughter, Theodosia; the only holy influence in his tempestuous life.

And Theodosia had been lost at sea. No authentic word of her, or of the ship that carried her, has ever been received. Burr had spent every day for months pacing the Battery sea wall, straining those uncanny black eyes of his for glimpses of her ship. He had spent every dollar he could lay hands on in sending for news of her. And then he had given up hope. This had been long before.

His daughter dead, his political hopes blasted, his country's gates barred against him, he dragged out a miserable life in Europe. Then, after years of absence, he slipped into the United States in disguise.

The first news of his return came in a New York newspaper announcement that "Colonel Aaron Burr has opened law offices on the second floor of 23 Nassau Street." The government made no move to deport him. Clients by the dozen flocked to take advantage of his brilliant legal intellect. Poverty, in a breath, gave place to prosperity.

This was in the spring of 1833, a scant three years after Papa Jumel's sudden demise. Tidings came to Betty that her old adorer, after so long a lapse of time, was back in New York. And across the gap of years came memories of his mesmeric eyes, his wonderful voice—the eyes and voice no woman could resist—the inspired manner of his love-making. And Betty went to him.

Throughout his love-starred life it was Burr's solemn declaration that never once did he take a single step out of his path to win any woman; that all his myriad conquests came to him unsought. Probably this was true. There are worse ways of bagging any form of game than by "still hunting." Perhaps there are few better.

At all events, down Broadway in her France-built coach rolled Betty Jumel—tall, blond, statuesque as in the Betty Bowen days when Peter Croix had "bought a book for his friends to read." She called on Burr, ostensibly to consult him about a legal matter involving a real-estate deal. But Burr understood. Burr always understood.

He saw, too, that Betty was still fair to look upon and that she had lost little of her charm. By common report he knew she was egregiously rich. He himself was wizened, white of hair, and seventy-eight years old. Poverty, griefs, bitter disappointments had sadly broken him. Save for his eyes and voice and brain, there was little about him to remind Betty of the all-conquering and dapper little Lothario of forty years back. Yet, as he listened and looked, she loved him. Yes, there is a goodly assortment of hornets' nests wherein a fool may run his head without visiting the same nest twice.

A few days after her call at his office, Betty gave one of her renowned dinner parties. It was "in honor of Colonel Burr." The guest of honor carried all before him that evening. The people who had come to stare at him as an escaped arch-criminal went home wholly enslaved by his magnetic charm. Aaron Burr had come to his own again.

In saying good night to his hostess, Burr lingered after the other guests had trundled off cityward in their carriages. Then, taking his leave with bared head, there in the moonlight on the steps of the Jumel mansion, he dropped lightly to one knee and raised Betty's hand to his lips.

"Madam," he breathed, the merciful moonlight making him for the moment his young and irresistible

self again, "madam, I give you my hand. My heart
has long been yours."

It was a pretty, old-world speech. Betty thought—
or affected to think—it meant nothing. But it
was the opening gun of a swift campaign. Day
after day thereafter, Burr neglected his fast-growing law business to drive out to the house above
the river. Every day he drew the siege lines closer to
the citadel.

At length he asked Betty to marry him. With a
final glimmer of common sense, she refused. He went
away. Betty feared he would not come back. But
he did. He came back the very next day—July 1,
1833. And with him in the carriage was another old
man—the Reverend Doctor Bogart, who had per-
formed the marriage ceremony for Burr and the latter's
first wife.

To the butler who admitted them, Burr gave a curt
message for Madame Jumel, asking that she come
down to them at once in the drawing-room. Wondering, she obeyed.

"Madam," said Burr, by way of salutation, "I have
come here today to marry you. Pray get ready at
once!"

Betty indignantly refused, and all but ordered her
suitor and the clergyman from the house. Then Burr
began to talk. The consummate eloquence that had
swayed prejudiced juries to his will, the love pleas that
no woman had been able to hear unmoved, the match-

less skill at argument that had made him master of men and women alike—all were brought into play.

An aged, discredited, half-impoverished failure was asking a beautiful and enormously rich woman to be his wife. Those were the cold facts. But cold facts had a way of vanishing before Aaron Burr's personality. Perhaps the greatest lingual triumph of his seventy-eight years was won when this feeble old man broke down within half an hour all Betty's defenses of coquetry and of sanity as well.

At last she ran from the room, murmuring that she would "decide and let him know." Burr sank back wearily in his chair. The victory was won. He knew it.

A little later Betty reappeared at the head of the stairs. She was resplendent in a gown of thick, stiff, dove-colored satin, and she glittered with a thousand jewels. Burr, lightly as a boy, ran up the stairs to meet her. Without a word she took his proffered arm. Together they walked to where the clergyman, stationed by Burr, awaited them. And they were married—super-woman and super-man. I know of no other instance in the History of Love where two such consummate heart breakers became man and wife.

It would be pleasant to record that the magnetic old couple walked hand and hand into the sunset; that their last years were spent together in the light of the afterglow. Here was a husband after Betty's own heart. Here was a wife to excite the envy of all Burr's friends, to rehabilitate him socially and financially. It seemed an ideal union.

But the new-wed pair did none of the things that any optimist would predict, that any astute student of human nature would set down in a novel about them. Before the honeymoon was over, they were quarreling like cat and dog. About money, of course. Burr sold some stock for his wife, and neglected to turn over the proceeds to her. She asked for the money. He curtly replied:

"Madam, this time you are married to a **man.** A man who will henceforth take charge of all your business affairs."

Betty's temper had never, at best, threatened to rob the patient Griselda of her laurels. Men had been her slaves, not her masters. She had no fancy for changing the lifelong conditions. So, in a blaze of anger, she not only demanded her money, but hinted very strongly that Colonel Burr was little better than a common fortune hunter.

Burr ordered her to go to her room and stay there until she could remember the respect due from a wife to her husband. She made a hot retort to the effect that the house was hers, and that, but for her wealth, Burr was a mere outcast and beggar.

Burr, without a word, turned and left the house. This was just ten days after the wedding. He went to New York and took up his abode in his former Duane Street lodgings. Betty, scared and penitent, went after him.   There was a reconciliation, and he came back.

But soon there was another squabble about money. And Betty, in another tantrum, went to a lawyer and brought suit to take the control of her fortune out of her husband's hands.   Again Burr left his new home, vowing he would never return.

The poor old fellow, once more cast upon his own resources, and self-deprived of the luxuries his wife's money had brought him, fell ill.   When Betty, in another contrite fit, went to plead with him to come back, she found him delirious.   She had him carried out to the mansion, and for weeks nursed him right tenderly.

But when he came again to his senses, Burr would not speak to his wife.   The moment he was able to get out of bed, he left the house.   Betty never saw him again.   Not very long afterward he died, in a Staten Island hotel—alone, unmourned, he who had been the darling of women.

Did Betty mourn her husband emeritus?   Not noticeably.   She was not of the type that mourns.   Before Burr was fairly under the sod, she was flirting gayly and was demanding and receiving the same admiration that had always been hers.   She sought to make people forget that she had ever been Mrs. Burr, and she asked them to call her, once more, "Madame Jumel."   She dazzled New York with a mammoth flower fete in the summer of 1837; and once more,

heedless of people's opinions, ruled as queen of New
York's little social realm.

And so the years sped on, until the super-woman
of other days could no longer fight off that incurable
disease, old age. American men no longer vied for
her favors. She decided that American men's taste
for beauty had been swallowed up by commercialism.
And she went again to Paris, where, she remembered,
men had never ceased to sue for her love.

This was in 1853. Louis Napoleon had just made
himself "Napoleon III., Emperor of the French." He
had a way, in the days of his power, of forgetting those
who had befriended him when he was down-at-the-heel
exile, and of snubbing former friends who were so
foolish as to claim present notice on the ground of past
favors.

But he made a notable exception in the case of
Madame Jumel. He received her with open arms, gave
a court ball in honor of her return to Paris, and in
every way treated her almost as if she had been a visiting sovereign. One likes to think his overworked re-
cording angel put all this down in large letters on the
credit side of Napoleon the Little's celestial ledger
page. Heaven knows there was plenty of blank space
on that side of the page for any such entries.

But on Betty herself the effect of all this adoration
was decidedly startling. Treated like a queen, she
grew to believe she **was** a queen. The razor-keen wits
that had stood by her so gallantly for three-quarters

of a century or more were dulling. Her mind began wandering helplessly in the realms of fancy. An odd phase of her mental decay was that she took to babbling incessantly of Aaron Burr—whose name she had not spoken in years—and she seemed to forget that she had ever met a man named Jumel.

She came back to the old house on the hill, overlooking the Harlem. The stream was no longer as pastoral and deserted as in earlier days, and houses and cottages had begun to spring up all around the confines of the mansion's grounds. New York was slowly creeping northward.

But it is to be doubted that Betty realized the change. She was a queen; no less a queen because she ruled an imaginary kingdom.

She declared that her position as a sovereign demanded a body of household troops. So she hired a bodyguard of twenty soldiers, dressed them in gay uniforms, and placed them on duty around the house. She increased her staff of servants to an amazing degree. She assumed regal airs. Every visitor was announced as if entering the presence of royalty. Betty no longer "received callers." Instead, she "held audiences." Yearly she journeyed in state to Saratoga, with a retinue of fifty servants and "officers of the household."

Money went like water in the upkeep of the queenly establishment. The once-boundless Jumel wealth that she had helped to amass began to shrink under the strain.   Yet so great was that fortune that more than a million dollars of it was left after she died.

New York was kind.   Men who had loved Betty, women who had been envied because of her friendship for them, rallied about her now, in her dotage, and helped her keep up the pitiable farce of queenship.

And in the mansion on the hill, on July 16, 1865, she fell asleep.   A score of New York's foremost men were her honorary pallbearers.   And all society made, for the last time, the long journey to Harlem to honor her memory.

So died Betty Bowen—Betty Jumel—Betty Burr—whatever you prefer to call her.   She was New York's first and greatest official heart breaker.   She was doubly fortunate, too, in missing the average old-super-woman's realization of having outgrown her wonder-charm.   For when her life book of beauty and power and magnetism closed, Delusion tenderly took up the tale.   And through a fairyland of imagined admiration and regal rank, Betty tottered happily to the very end.

CHAPTER SIX

ADRIENNE LECOUVREUR

THE "ACTRESS HEART QUEEN"

S HE was an exlaundress, and the daughter of a hatter.

He was an ideal dime-novel hero, and the son of a king. She was all spirit. He was all body. And their love story is, perhaps, the strangest of its sort in the sad annals of hearts.

(Their great-great-granddaughter, by the way, was George Sand—a four-generation throwback of the nameless super-woman trait.)

Having thus rhapsodied with the hope of catching the reader's attention, one may ring up the curtain on a romance whose compelling interest cannot be spoiled by the most bungling writing.

She was Adrienne Lecouvreur; and like the bulk of history's super-women, she sprang from the masses. Her childhood was spent in beating against the bars behind which her eagle spirit was locked. At fourteen she joined a road company; and within a few years she was acclaimed as the greatest actress the world had thus far known.

As a **comedienne** she was a failure. It was in tragedy that she soared to untouched heights. And her life, from cradle to unmarked grave, was one long, sustained tragedy of love. Or, rather, of loves. For she had divers harsh experiences before the last great love flashed upon her.

It was at Lille, while she was still in her apprenticeship as an actress, that Adrienne met a young baron; a captain in the local garrison. He loved her, and he was her first love. It was not the custom of the early eighteenth century for a French noble to propose marriage to a former laundress who was playing utility parts in a third-rate road show. Probably there was no precedent for it. And such a proposal would have been a waste of windy words, at best. For neither the king nor the man's parents would have allowed it to lead to marriage.

Yet—or perhaps because of it—the baron asked Adrienne Lecouvreur to be his wife. She was in the seventh paradise of first love. It was all turning out the way it did in plays. And plays were, thus far, Adrienne's chief guidebook of life. So the prettily staged engagement began; with roseate light effects.

Before Adrienne had time for disillusionment, the baron died. In the first grief—she was at an age when every tragedy is absolutely permanent and irrevocable

—the luckless girl tried to kill herself. Her kindly fellow actors took turns in watching her and in abstracting unobtrusively any lethal weapons that might chance to be within her reach. And at last Youth came to the rescue; permanent heartbreak being too mighty a feat for sixteen.

Adrienne fell to referring to the baron's death as her life tragedy, not yet realizing that the affair was but an insignificant curtain raiser.

By and by another nobleman crossed her horizon. He was Philippe le Ray. And for the moment he fascinated Adrienne. Once more there was a hope— or she thought there was—of a marriage into the aristocracy. Then, just as everything seemed to be along smoothly, she threw away her possible chances with both hands.

Into the road company came a new recruit, Clavel by name. You will not find him in the shining records of the French stage, nor under the "Cs" in any encyclopedia. His name has been picked in history's museum solely from the fact that he jilted Adrienne Lecouvreur.

Philippe le Ray was promptly shelved for the new love. And with him Adrienne sacrificed all her supposed chances of wealth, rank, and ease; for the sake of a penniless actor, and for love.

She became engaged to Clavel. They planned to marry as soon as their joint earnings would permit, and to tour France as co-stars. Or, if the public preferred, with Clavel as star, and with Adrienne as an adoringly humble member of the cast.

Early in the affair, Clavel found a better-paying position in another company. Adrienne urged him to accept it, for the temporary parting promised to bring nearer the day of their marriage. And Clavel, to please her, took the offer.

So, again, Adrienne found herself alone. But it was a loneliness that vibrated with hope. It was at this time that she chose for herself a motto, which thereafter emblazoned her letters and lingerie.

It was, **"Que Faire Au Monde Sans Aimer?"** ("What is living without loving?") She was soon to learn the grim answer to the challenge-query she so gayly hurled at fate.

Clavel's letters grew few. They waned in warmth. Odd rumors with which the theater world has ever been rife began to reach Adrienne. And at last she wrote her absent lover a missive that has been numbered by **cognoscenti** among the great love letters of the ages. Here it is, in part—a halting translation:

> I scarce know what to believe, from your neglect. But be certain always that I love you for yourself a hundred times more dearly than on my own account. Oh, love me, dear, as I shall forever love you! That is all I ask from life.
>
> But don't promise to, unless you can keep your word. Your welfare is far more precious to me than my own. So always follow the course that seems most pleasant to you. If ever I lose you and you are still happy, I shall have the joy of knowing I have not been a bar to your happiness.

The worthy Clavel took Adrienne at her word. He proceeded to "follow the course that seemed most pleasant to him"—by breaking the engagement and marrying a lesser woman who had a **dot** of several thousand francs. He explained his action by saying that he must look out for his own future, and that Adrienne had no prospects of success on the stage.

And thus the thrifty actor passes out of history. Thus, too, he lost a future chance to handle the funds of Europe's richest actress, and of starring as her husband. Peace to his puny soul!

Adrienne Lecouvreur no longer clamored to die. She was older now—nearly twenty. And the latest blow hardened instead of crushing her. By this time the girlish chrysalis had been shed and a gloriously beautiful woman had emerged. Already she was hailed as the "Actress Heart Queen." Men were straining the vocabulary of imbecility to coin phrases for her.

And for the first and last time in her career, Adrienne resolved to capitalize her charms. It was the one adventuress-moment in all her story. And the Hand that ever guided her course picked her up and set her back, very hard and very promptly, in the destined path of tragedy from which she had tried to stray.

Stinging and heart-dead from Clavel's desertion. she listened to the vows of the Comte de Klinglin. He was rich; he was a soldier of note; and Adrienne was no longer the world-innocent child of her first engagement days. She played her cards with the skill of a perfect actress. From mere flirtation, the count advanced to the point of worshiping her.

De Klinglin besought her to marry him. And with seeming reluctance, she yielded. She even pointed out a way by which they might evade royal and family law by emigrating for a time to some other country. and then, by judicious bribery, arranging a return and a reinstatement. De Klinglin entered eagerly into the plan.

Then, on the very eve of their proposed wedding, the count deserted her and married an heiress. Decidedly, the Hand was guiding Adrienne against every effort or desire of her own.

This latest blow to pride and to new-born ambition was the turning point in Adrienne Lecouvreur's road. It changed her from a professional beauty into an inspired actress.

She threw herself into her work with a tragic intensity bred of her own sorrows. She turned her back on social distractions, and on' everything that came between her and success. Her acting as well as her beauty became the talk of the provinces. Word of her prowess drifted to Paris, the Mecca of eighteenth-century actor-folk. A Paris manager came to see her act. and he at once engaged her.

In 1717, when she was twenty-three, she burst unheralded upon the French metropolis. In a night, Paris was at her feet. Almost at once, she was made a leading woman of the **Comedie Francaise;** where, for thirteen years, she reigned, undisputed sovereign of the French stage.

Never before had such acting been witnessed or even imagined. It was a revelation. Up to this time French actors had mouthed their words noisily and grandiloquently, reciting the Alexandrine or otherwise metrical lines—wherein practically all the classic plays of the period, except some of Moliere's, were written— in a singsong chant that played sad havoc with the sense.

Incidentally, the costuming—as you may see from contemporary cuts—was a nightmare. And when a character on the stage was not declaiming or dramatically listening, he usually stood stock-still in a statuesque attitude, staring into blank space, with the look of an automaton.

All this seems ridiculous to us; but it had come straight down as an almost inviolable "classic tradition" from the ancient Greek drama, which had been more a series of declamations than a vital play.

Yes, Adrienne Lecouvreur was a revelation to Paris. On the stage her voice was as soft and musical as it was penetrating. Instead of intoning a pompous monologue, she spoke her lines as people in real life spoke. Her emotions were keenly human. Every syllable and every shade of voice meant something.

Without sacrificing the poetry of the rhymed couplets, she put the breath of life and of conversational meaning into them.   She dressed the characters she played in the way such persons might reasonably have been supposed to dress.   She made them a joy to the eye instead of an insult to the intelligence.   And when she was not speaking, she was forever acting; introducing a million bits of byplay to replace the old statuesque poses.

She had lived.   And she put the breath of that life into her work.   This seems simple enough to us in these days of stage realism.   But it was a wonder-breeding novelty to France.   Adrienne revolutionized acting, diction, and costuming.   Paris acclaimed her as a genius; which abused term was for once well applied.

Men of rank clamored for introductions to her. They plotted, and sighed, and bribed, and killed one another for her favor.   But for them all she had one stereotyped answer; an answer that waxed historic through many firm repetitions:

"Love is a folly which I detest!"

Which, in conjunction with her motto, "What is living without loving?" throws a sidelight on Adrienne's ideas of life at the moment.

Not only did she revolutionize the stage, but she was the first actress to be taken up by society.   Not only the foremost men in France, but their wives as well, threw open to her the magic doors of the Faubourg Saint-Germain.

Old Philippe the Regent was misgoverning France just then; and to say that his court was morally rotten would be gross flattery. The unapproachable Lecouvreur was thus a freak, as well as a delight. Like the good, old, overworked "breath of mountain air in a slum," this loveless genius swept through the palaces of Paris and Versailles. A hundred nobles longed for her favor. Not one could boast that he had so much as kissed her lips. Here is her picture, sketched from the **Mercure,** of 1719:

Without being tall, she is exquisitely formed and has an air of distinction. No one on earth has greater charm. Her eyes speak as eloquently as her lips, and often they supply the place of words. In brief, I can compare her only to a flawless miniature. Her head is well poised on shapely shoulders. Her eyes are full of fire; her mouth is pretty; her nose slightly aquiline. Her face is wonderfully adapted to express joy, tenderness, pity, fear, sorrow.

And Adrienne? Her opinion of all this adulation is summed up in one sentence from a letter she wrote:

I spend three-fourths of my time in doing what bores me.

Among her maddest admirers was a wizened, monkey-faced youth who even then was writing anarchistic doctrines that one day were to help shake France's worm-eaten old monarchy to its fall.

He was Francois Marie Arouet. But for reasons best known to himself, he preferred to be known simply as "Voltaire"—a name to which he had no right

whatever, but by which alone history remembers him.
Voltaire was Adrienne Lecouvreur's adoring slave.
She treated him only as a dear friend; but she loved
to hear his vitriolic anathemas on government, the
aristocracy, and theology. He was in the midst of one
of these harangues, at her rooms one evening, when
the Chevalier de Rohan—bearer of the proudest name
in all Europe—sauntered in. He eyed the monkeylike Voltaire in amused disfavor; then drawled, to no
one in particular:

"Who is this young man who talks so loud?"

"A young man, sir," retorted Voltaire, "who is not
forced to stagger along under a name far too great for
him; but who manages to secure respect for the name
he has."

De Rohan's tasseled cane swung aloft. Adrienne
tactfully prevented its fall by collapsing in a stage
faint. But the incident did not close there. Next day
Voltaire was set upon by ruffians in Rohan's pay, and
beaten half to death.

The victim did not complain. There was no justice
for a commoner, in France at that time, against a
member of the **haute noblesse.** So Voltaire contented
himself by going to a fencing master and practicing for
a year or more in the use of the small-sword.

At the end of that period, he challenged Rohan
to mortal combat. Rohan professed to regard the
challenge as a piece of insolence, and, through royal
favor, had Voltaire, sent, by **lettre de cachet,** to the

Bastille. There was no chance for redress. And, on his release, Voltaire prudently let the feud drop.

At the perihelion of Adrienne's Dianalike sway over French hearts, a new social lion arrived in Paris. He was Maurice, Comte de Saxe, born of a morganatic union between a German countess and Augustus the Strong, King of Poland. (Augustus, by the way, was the parent of no less than one hundred and sixty-three children—an interesting record even in those days of large families, and one that should have gone far toward earning for him the title of "Father of his Country.")

Saxe came to Paris crowned with laurels won as a dashing military leader, as a fearless duelist, and as an irresistible heart breaker. He had won, by sheer bravery and strategic skill, the rank of Marshal. He was of the "man on horseback" type over whom crowds go wild.

The new hero was a giant in stature, strikingly handsome, and so strong that in one hand he could crush a horseshoe into a shapeless lump. He was a paladin —Ajax, Don Juan, Tamerlane, Mark Antony, Baldur, all rolled into one. He was a glorious animal, high of spirits and of hopes, devoid of fear and of the finer feelings. A Greek god—or whatever you will. And about him hung the glamour of countless conquests on the battlefield and in love.

That such a man should have turned Paris' head was inevitable. Equally natural was it that Paris

women should make fools of themselves over him.
But why so gross and unintellectual a wooer should
have made the very slightest impression on a character
like Adrienne Lecouvreur's must be relegated to the
"mystery of choice" collection of riddles.

Yet, at sight, she, who for years had scoffed at passion, and who had so often declared her heart was
dead, felt that she had met the love of her life.

She gave her revivified heart and her whole soul
into Maurice de Saxe's keeping. forever and ever.
There were no reservations.   Hers was a love that
could die only with her life.   The former affairs were
to her as half-forgotten dreams.   Saxe, and Saxe alone,
held her love; held it as no other man had been able
to.

Adrienne at first dazzled Saxe—as a tropic butterfly
might dazzle a champion bulldog.   The dazzle soon
wore off; but it left behind a comfortable feeling of
affection, of admiration, of gratified vanity that he
alone had been chosen by her, out of all the world of
suitors.

With the deft hands of a sculptor, Adrienne Lecouvreur molded Saxe's rough nature.   She refined
him; taught him to replace the ways of the camp by
those of civilization; made him less of a beast and
more of a man; showed him how to think.

All of which added to the man's popularity with
other women; which was the sole reward Adrienne
reaped for her educative efforts.

Saxe was notoriously untrue to her. In his rages he berated her as a cabby might have scolded his drunken wife. He used his power over her to raise himself in others' esteem. In short, he was wholly selfish throughout, and he gruffly consented to accept Adrienne's worship as his just due.

But Adrienne's love merely waxed stronger and brighter under such abominable treatment. She lived for Saxe alone.

The Duchy of Courland lost its duke. His place was to be filled by election. And with the dukedom went the hand of a Russian princess, whose face Saxe unchivalrously compared to a Westphalia ham.

Saxe's ambition awoke. In his veins ran royal blood. He wanted to be a duke and the husband of a princess. He entered as candidate in the contest. Lack of money, for judicious bribes to the free and incorruptible electors, stood in his way. He went, as ever in trouble, to Adrienne. And, as ever, she rose to the occasion.

She knew that, as Duke of Courland, he could not see her again, or be within several hundred miles of her. She knew, too, that, by helping him with the dukedom, she was helping to give him to another woman. A lesser love than hers would have rebelled at either possibility.

But Adrienne's love for Saxe was that which not only casts out fear, but casts out self along with it. She sold every piece of jewelry and every costly dress and stick of furniture in her possession, borrowed money right and left, and mortgaged her salary at the Comedie Francaise.

The net result was fifteen thousand dollars, which she gladly handed over to Saxe for the expenses of his campaign.   With these sinews of war, Saxe hastened to Courland.   There he remained for a year; working hard for his election; making love to the ham-faced princess; fighting like a Norse berserker in battle after battle.

He was elected duke.   But Russia refused to sanction the election.   At the head of a handful of fellow adventurers, Saxe went on fighting; performing prodigies of personal valor and strength in conflicts against overwhelming odds.   But at last he was hopelessly beaten in battle, and still more hopelessly outpointed in the game of politics.   And back he came to Paris—a failure.

Adrienne used every art and charm to make him forget his misfortunes and find happiness once more in her love.   He treated her overtures as a surly schoolboy might treat those of an over-affectionate little sweetheart.

He consented to be petted and comforted by the woman who adored him.   But he wreaked in her the ill-temper bred of his defeat.   For example, he professed to believe her untrue to him.   He was furiously jealous—or pretended to be.   And he accused her of the infidelity he had himself a thousand times practiced.

Poor Adrienne, aghast at such insane charges,

vainly protested her innocence and her utter love for him. One of her letters to Saxe, during this dark hour, has been preserved. It begins:

I am worn out with grief. I have wept this livelong night. It is foolish of me; since I have nothing wherewith to reproach myself. But I cannot endure severity from you. I am suspected, accused by you. Oh, how can I convince you—you who alone can wound my heart?

In the midst of this wretched misunderstanding came a crumb of comfort to the luckless woman—albeit the incident that caused it led also, indirectly, to her death.

Francoise de Lorraine, Duchesse de Bouillon, fell violently in love with Saxe, and did not hesitate to tell him so. Saxe laughed in her face, and hinted that he cared too much for Adrienne Lecouvreur just then to be interested in any one else. It was not the truth, for his love for Adrienne had never served as an obstacle to any other of his myriad amours. But it served to rebuff the duchesse, who did not interest him, and to make Adrienne very, very happy when he repeated to her the conversation. As a by-product, it threw the duchesse into a frame of mind described by Congreve in his line about the Gehennalike fury of a woman scorned.

A few days after this—in July, 1729—Adrienne received an anonymous note asking her to be at a certain corner of the Luxembourg Gardens at eleven o'clock the following morning. Being quite without fear, and not at all without curiosity, she went.

No, she was not set upon by masked assassins. She found awaiting her nothing more formidable than a pale and badly scared young man in clerical garb.

The clerical youth introduced himself as the Abbe Bouret, a hanger-on of the Bouillon household. Bouret told Adrienne that the duchesse had bribed him heavily to send her rival a box of poisoned bonbons, with a note saying the candies were the gift of an unknown and humble admirer.

The abbe had seen Adrienne a few nights earlier at the theater. So struck had be been by the gentleness and beauty of her face that he could not carry out his murderous commission. Hence the warning.

Adrienne took the abbe, and the candy, too, straight to the police. A bonbon was fed to a street dog. The animal, screaming and writhing in agony. died within fifteen minutes. This seemed, even to the eighteenth-century Paris police, a fairly good proof of the duchesse's guilt.

Naturally, they did not arrest her grace. But they put certain respectful queries to her. Strangely enough, the duchesse indignantly denied that she had tried to poison Adrienne.

Bouret, cross-examined, stuck determinedly to his story. So, through the Bouillon influence, he was

thrown into prison and was kept there in solitary con-
finement, in a damp and unlighted dungeon, with
occasional torture, until he saw the error of his ways,
and confessed that his charge had been a lie.   Thus
was the faultless Duchesse de Bouillon triumphantly
cleared of an unjust accusation.

The duchesse celebrated her vindication by
attending the theater, one night when Adrienne
Lecouvreur was playing in "Phedre."   The duchesse
sat in a stage box and mockingly applauded her
rival.

Adrienne paid no overt heed at first to her
presence.   But when she came to the scene in which
Phedre expresses to **Œnone** her contempt for a certain
class of women, Adrienne turned her back on the
wondering **Œnone,** strode to the footlights, and, her
blazing eyes seizing and gripping the duchesse's, declaimed directly to her **Phedre's** lines:

"I know my own faults; but I am not one of those brazen
women who, calm even in the exposure of their crimes, can
face the world without a blush."

The duchesse shrank back as if she had been lashed
across the face.   Shielding her eyes with her hands,
she ran, shuddering, from the theater.

Scribe's play, "Adrienne Lecouvreur," and the opera
of the same title, make much of this episode.   So did
eighteenth-century Paris.   Folk openly declared that

the Duchesse de Bouillon would not long rest impotent under so public an insult.   And they were right.

Whether the poison was sent in a bouquet, as contemporary writers declared, or in some other form, Adrienne was suddenly stricken by mortal illness.

Less than half a century had passed since the dying King Charles had "lived a week in spite of the best physicians in England."   And the science of medicine had crept forward but few hesitating steps in the past forty-five years.   Poor, stricken Adrienne did not even need the best malpractice in France to help her to her grave.

Doctors great and doctors greater—the quacks of the Rive Gauche and the higher-priced quacks of court and Faubourg—all stood in turn at the dying girl's bedside and consulted gravely in Latin; while Saxe raged at them and cursed them for a parcel of solemn nincompoops—which they were.

After a time they all trooped away, these long-faced men of pill and potion.   They confessed they could find no remedy.   They could not so much as name the ailment.   At least, they did not—aloud.   For the memory of the first poison scandal and its revealer's fate was still fresh in men's minds.

And after the doctors came the priest; a priest hastily summoned by the infidel Voltaire, who had been crying outside the death-chamber door.

The priest was among the most bigoted of his kind. In his eyes, the victim was not the reigning beauty of

Paris, but a sinning creature who had defied God's laws by going on the stage.

Theology in those days barred actors and actresses from the blessings of the Church.

Yet, bigoted as was this particular priest, he was not wholly heartless. The weeping little monkeylike man crouched on the stairs outside the door may have touched his heart; for Voltaire could be wondrous eloquent and persuasive. Or the red-eyed, raging giant on his knees at the bedside may have appealed to his pity; almost as much as did the lovely white face lying so still there among the pillows. At all events, the good priest consented to strain a point.

If Adrienne would adjure her allegiance to the stage and banish all earthly thoughts, he would absolve her and would grant her the rite of Extreme Unction.

"Do you place your hope in the God of the Universe?" he intoned.

Slowly the great dark eyes—already wide with the Eternal Mystery—turned from the priest to the sobbing giant who knelt at the opposite side of her bed. Adrienne Lecouvreur stretched out her arms toward Saxe, for the last of many thousand times. Pointing at her weeping lover, she whispered to the priest:

"There is my Universe, my Hope, my God!"

The good priest scuttled away in pious horror. Adrienne Lecouvreur sank back upon the pillows, dead—and unabsolved.

That night—acting on a strong hint from the

Bouillon family, who had heard that Voltaire intended to demand an autopsy—the police carried Adrienne's body away in a cab, and buried it in a bed of quick-lime.

For nearly two long months, Maurice, Comte de Saxe, scarcely looked at another woman.

CHAPTER SEVEN.

CLEOPATRA

"THE SERPENT OF OLD NILE"

SOME thirty-five years ago, in the north Jersey village of Pompton, the township undertaker's barn burned down. It was a spectacular midnight fire. All the natives turned out to view it. Dominie Jansen even hinted, I remember, that it was a visitation on the community for some of his neighbors' sins. Whereat, Lem Saulsbury took the pledge —for the eighth time that year.

Well, the next week, when the Pompton **Clarion** appeared, no mention was made of the fire—the only event of intense human interest, by the way, since Joel Binswanger, the official local sot, six months earlier had, at the village tavern, swallowed a half-pint flask of carbolic acid—set aside for cleaning the brasses— under the conviction that it was applejack. Joel had complained of a rough throat and an unwonted taste in his mouth for days afterward. The Clarion editor, taken to task for printing nothing about the fire, excused the omission by saying;

"What'd 'a been the use of writing the story?
Everybody knows about it."

That's all there is to the anecdote. Yes, I've heard
better, myself. I've even heard the same one better
told. It serves, though, as a fitting preamble to my
story about Cleopatra.

"Everybody knows about it."

Who can say anything about her that you have not
heard? Perhaps I can. Probably not. Will you
be patient with me, and, even as tourists visit
European shrines to verify their Baedekers, read this
story to verify what you have always known?
Cleopatra cannot be omitted from any super-woman
series. And I will make her as interesting as I know
how.

Personally, I belive the Pomptonians would far
rather have read about that barn blaze, which they had
seen, than about the conflagration of a whole foreign
metropolis.

At sixteen—in 52 B. C.—Cleopatra's known career
as a heartbreaker began; although there are rumors
of more than one still earlier affair, with Egyptian
nobles as their heroes.

She was the daughter of Ptolemy Auletes—Ptolemy
the Piper—cordially hated ruler of Egypt. Cleopatra
and her baby brother, young Ptolemy, nominally
shared the throne for a time. They were both
children. They ruled much as the baby "drives" when
he holds the reins of the horse at whose head is the

hostler's guiding hand. All manner of adventurers—both native and Greek—were the real rulers.

One of these factions drove Cleopatra from the throne and from her capital at Alexandria, leaving the "triple Uræus crown," with its mystic lotus adornments, on the head of baby Ptolemy alone.

The crown was the only fragment of actual kingship the child possessed. The power and the graft lay in the hands of a trio of industriously grasping Greek adventurers.

Cleopatra, meantime, out in the cold, schemed to regain her place on the double throne, and, even at that early age, amused herself in the interim by planning the tortures she would wreak on little Ptolemy when her turn should come.

While she was casting about for means to outwit the Greeks, and seeking means to buy up a mercenary army of invasion, she learned that Julius Cæsar, an elderly Roman of vast repute as a conqueror, had come to Alexandria at the head of a few legions, on a mission of diplomacy.

Cleopatra may have known little of men's strength, but already she was a profound student of their weaknesses.

She began to ask questions about Cæsar. Brushing away (as immaterial if true), her scared native attendants' statements that he had the body of an elephant, the head of a tiger, and the claws of a dragon, and that he fed on prisoners served raw, she pumped one or two exiled Romans and gleaned an inkling of the conqueror's history.

With the details of Cæsar's Gallic invasion, his crushing of Pompey, and his bullying of semihostile fellow Romans, she did not in the least concern herself. What most interested Cleopatra were the following domestic revelations:

He had been married at least four times, and three of his wives were still living. Cossutia, the wife of his youth, he had divorced by law because he had been captivated by the charms of one Cornelia, whom he had forthwith married, and who had died before he had had time to name her successor.

Next in order he had wed Pompeia; and, on the barest rumor of indiscretion on her part, had announced dramatically: "Cæsar's wife must be above suspicion!" and had divorced her to marry his present spouse, Calpurnia.

The interstices between these unions had been garnished with many a love episode. Adamant as he was toward men. Cæsar was far from being an anchorite where women were concerned; and he had the repute of being unswervingly loyal to the woman whom he, at the time, chanced to love.

This scurrilous information was quite enough for Cleopatra. She had her plans accordingly. She would see Cæsar. More to the point, she would be seen by Cæsar. But how? Cæsar was in Alexandria, the stronghold of her enemies. It would mean capture

and subsequent death for Cleopatra to be found in the
city.   Yet she planned not only to enter Alexandria,
but to make her first appearance before Cæsar in a
way designed to catch his attention and more than
friendly interest from the very start.

Julius Cæsar sat in the great audience hall of the
Alexandria palace, whose use he had commandeered
as his temporary headquarters.   Behind him stood his
guards; heavy armored, tanned of face; short, thick
swords at hip.   Before his dais trailed a procession of
folk who hated him as starkly as they feared him.

They were Egyptians with favors to ask, and they
bore gifts to indorse their pleas.   They were Greeks
who sought to outwit the barbarian victor, or to trick
him into the granting of concessions.   One by one the
suppliants crawled past, each crying out an appeal or
a grievance.   Nearly every one made a peace offering,
until the mass of gifts was stacked high on the stone
floor of the audience hall.

Presently entered two black porters, (strapping
Nubian giants), who bore lightly between them a roll of
rare Persian carpet.   They halted, laid down their
burden on the floor at Cæsar's feet, fell on their knees
in obeisance, and—waited.   On the floor lay the roll
of priceless weave, no one coming forward to make
the rich gift an excuse for the urging of some boon.

Cæsar grew inquisitive.   He leaned forward to ex-
amine the tight-folded, shimmering rug more carefully.
As he did so, the folds were suddenly flung aside, and

a girl leaped to her feet from among them. Thus had Cleopatra entered Alexandria. Thus had she penetrated to Cæsar's presence. Thus, too, by her craft and daring, had she won the attention of the man whose daring and craft had conquered the world.

Cæsar stared in delighted interest. He saw, standing gracefully—and wholly undraped—before him, a slender, red-haired girl, snub-nosed and of no special beauty. But, at a glance, this man who saw everything, saw, too, that she possessed an unnameable fascination—a magnetism—that was greater by far than that of any other woman he had known in all his fifty-eight years.

It was Julius Cæsar's first introduction to a superwoman; to the super-woman of super-women; to a woman beside whose snub-nosed, plain face, under its shock of red hair, the memory of the Roman beauties who had so often charmed his idle hours grew dim and confused.

Cleopatra, on her part, saw nothing so impressive as an elephant-tiger-dragon monster. She beheld a thin, undersized man, nearly sixty years old, hawk-nosed, inscrutable of eye, on whose thin gray locks, to mask his fast-growing baldness, rested a chaplet of laurel leaves.

This was the hero whose cunning and whose war genius had caused sceptered men to grovel at his feet, and had made stubborn republican Rome his cringing servant. But he was also the man whose weakness

was an attractive woman.   And on this weakness
Cleopatra at once proceeded to play.

Yet she speedily found that Cæsar's was but a surface weakness, and that beneath it lay iron.   Gladly
he consented to save her from her foes, and even in a
measure to let her punish such of those foes as were
of no use to him.   But as for making her the undisputed
Queen of Egypt and setting her triumphantly and in-
dependently on the throne of her ancestors, at Rome's
expense—he had not the remotest idea of doing that.

Nor could all her most bewildering blandishments
wring such a foolish concession from him.   He made
love to her—ardent love; but he did not let love inter-
fere in any way with politics.

Instead of carrying her to the throne, through seas
of her enemies' blood, he carried Cleopatra back to
Rome with him and, to the scandal of the whole city,
installed her in a huge marble villa there.

And there, no secret being made of Cæsar's infatuation for her, Cleopatra remained for the next few
years; indeed, until Cæsar's death.   There, too, Cæsar's
son, Cæsarion, was born; and with the boy's birth
came to Cleopatra the hope that Cæsar would will to
him all his vast estates and other wealth; which would
have been some slight compensation for the nonrestor-
ing of her throne.

While Cleopatra abode in Rome, more than one
man of world-fame bowed in homage before her.
For example, Lepidus—fat, stupid, inordinately rich,

fit dupe for cleverer politicians. Marcus Antonius, too,
—Cæsar's protege, and at this time a swaggering,
lovable, dissolute soldier-demagogue, whose fortunes
were so undissolubly fastened to Cæsar's that he, the
winner of a horde of women, dared not lift his eyes
to the woman Cæsar loved.

Among the rest—Marcus Brutus, snarling Casca, and
the others—came one more guest to the villa—a hard-
faced, cold-eyed youth whom Cleopatra hated. For
he was Caius Octavius, Cæsar's nephew and presump-
tive heir; the man who was, years hence, to be the
Emperor Augustus.

At length, one day, Rome's streets surged with hys-
terical mobs and factions. And news came to the
villa that Cæsar had been assassinated at the Forum.
Speedily an angry crowd besieged Cleopatra's house.

Now that the all-feared Cæsar no longer lived to
protect her, the people were keen to wreak punishment
on this foreign sorceress who had enmeshed the murdered man's brain, and had made him squander upon
her so much of the public wealth that might better have
gone into Roman pockets. Rome's new government,
too, at once ordered her expulsion from the city.

Cleopatra, avoiding the mob and dodging arrest, fled
from Rome with her son, her fortune, and her few
faithful serfs. One more hope was gone. For, instead
of leaving his money to Cæsarion, Cæsar, in his will,
had made the cold-eyed youth, Caius Octavius, his
heir.

Back to the East went Cleopatra, her sun of success temporarily in shadow. In semi-empty, if regal, state, she queened it for a time, her title barren, her real power in Egypt practically confined to her brain and to her charm. Nominal Queen of Egypt, she was still merely holding the reins, while iron-handed Rome strode at the horse's head.

From afar, she heard from time to time the tidings from Rome. The men who had slain Cæsar had themselves been overthrown. In their place Rome—and all the world—was ruled by a triumvirate made up of three men she well remembered—Octavius, Antony, and Lepidus.

The next news was that Antony and Octavius had painlessly extracted Lepidus from the combination, and were about to divide the government of the whole known world between themselves. Antony, to whom first choice was given, selected the eastern half for his share, leaving the west to Octavius.

Then came word that Antony was on his way toward Egypt; thither bound in order to investigate certain grave charges made by her subjects against Cleopatra herself.

Once more were the queen's throne and her life itself in peril. And once more she called upon her matchless power over men to meet and overcome the new menace. When Antony drew near to the capital, Cleopatra set forth to meet him; not with such an army as she might perchance have scraped together to oppose the invader, but relying solely on her own charms.

Antony by this time was well past his first youth. Here is Plutarch's word picture of him:

> He was of a noble presence. He had a goodly, thick beard, a broad forehead, and a crooked nose. And there appeared such a manly look in his countenance as is seen in the statues of Hercules. . . . And it is incredible what marvelous love he won.

Yes, and it is incredible into what messes that same "marvelous love," first and last, dragged him. He had a wondrous genius for war and for statesmanship; but ever, just as those qualities lifted him to eminence, some woman would drag him down. For instance, as a young man, his budding political hopes were wrecked by Flavia, a charmer who enslaved him. Later, Rome turned a deaf ear to the tales of his military glory because he chose to escort openly along the Appian Way a frail beauty named Cytheria, in a chariot drawn by four lions. In rapid succession he—like his idol, Cæsar—married four wives.

Flavia was the first—she who blasted his early statesmanship ambitions: next Antonia, from whom he soon separated; third, Fulvia, a shrew who made his home life a burden, and whose temper drove him far from her—not that he really needed such incentive.

But Fulvia loved him, as did all women. For when Cicero lay dead, she went to the orator's bier and thrust a bodkin through the once magic tongue; thus punishing the tongue, she explained, for its calumnies against her beloved husband.

Fulvia was not exactly a cozy-corner wife, as you, perhaps, have observed; yet, when she died, Antony was heartily sorry. He said so. At the time, he was far away from Rome and home—he had not taken Fulvia to Egypt with him—and was basking in Cleopatra's wiles. On a visit to Rome he next married Octavia, sister of Octavius. It was a state match. He speedily deserted her and hurried back to Egypt.

Antony—true lover and false husband, hero and fool, rake and statesman—had fifty sides to his character—and a woman was on every side. In times of peace he wallowed in the wildest dissipation, and spent vast fortunes without a second thought. In war, he was the idol of his men, carousing with them, sharing their hard fare and harder life, never losing their adoring respect, always the hero for whom they would blithely die.

And so back to the story.

Up the River Cydnus sailed Antony, bent on restoring order to Egypt and punishing the cruel Cleopatra. And down the River Cydnus to meet him came Cleopatra.

The barge, wherein lay the queen, had sails of purple and gold. It was propelled by oars of pure silver. Around the recumbent Cleopatra were beautiful attendants, clad—or unclad — as Nymphs, Graces,

Cupids. She herself wore, on her left ankle, a jeweled band in which was set a sacred scarab. That was the full extent of her costume.

At a single look, Antony forgot forever the punitive object of his journey to Egypt; forgot that he was ruler of half the world, and that he had the cleverness and power to oust Octavius from the other half, and to rule it all. He forgot everything except that he loved her, and was content to be her helpless and happy slave; that she was the supreme love of his thousand loves; that the world was well lost for such love as hers.

From that moment the old-time magnetic statesman and general, Marcus Antonius—with his shrewd plans for world conquest—was dead. In his place lived Mark Antony, prince of lovers; a man whose sole thought and aim in life consisted in worshipping at the bare feet of a red-haired, snub-nosed Egyptian woman.

Cæsar had loved Cleopatra—and won. Mark Antony loved her—and lost; lost everything—except perfect happiness. But for her, Antony might have striven night and day, with brain, will, and body, using his friends as sacrifices, employing a statesmanship that was black treachery, drenching all Europe in blood. But for Cleopatra, he might have done all this. He might, as a result, have ousted Octavius and made himself, for the minute, master of all the world—as a price for his years of racking toil—before some patriotic assassin got a chance to kill him.

Thanks to Cleopatra's malign influence, the old warrior spent his last years, instead, in a golden Fool's Paradise, whose joys have become historic. Wherefore, the schoolbooks hold up Antony as a horrible example of what a man may throw away, through folly.

I have tried, in the preceding few paragraphs, to re-enforce the school-books' teachings; to show that it is better to toil than to trifle, to sweat and suffer than to saunter through Arcady, to die dead-tired than to die divinely happy. I am sure I make the point clear. If I do not, the fault is not mine; and the sad, sad example of Antony has gone for naught.

They had a wonderful time there, in the Lotus Land, these two super-lovers. Each had had a host of earlier "affairs." But these now served merely as do the many rough "detail sketches" that work up at last into the perfected picture.

It was no heavy-tragedy romance. The two mature lovers had a saving sense of fun that sent them on larks worthy of high-school revelers. By night, they would go in disguise through the city, to revel unrecognized at some peasant wedding or orgy.

Once, the incognito Antony, on such an expedition, got a sound thrashing and a broken head from taking too prominent a part on a slum festivity. And Cleopatra never let him hear the last of it. That the all-conquering Marcus Antonius should have been beaten up by a crowd of Egyptian **fellaheen,** who trembled at the very mention of his name, struck her as the joke of the century.

She had a right lively sense of humor, had this "Serpent of Old Nile," as Antony playfully nicknamed her. And probably this sense of humor was one of the strongest fetters that bound to her the love veteran, who was sick of a succession of statelily humorless Roman beauties.

Cleopatra was forever playing practical jokes on her lover. Once, for example, as she and Antony sat fishing off their anchored barge in the Alexandria harbor, Antony wagered that he would make the first catch. Cleopatra took the bet. A moment afterward Antony felt a mighty tug at his line. With the zest of a born fisherman, he "drew in."

He brought to the surface, suspended from his hook, an enormous fish—dried, boned, and salted! Cleopatra had privily sent one of her divers over the far side of the barge to swim down and fasten the salted fish to her sweetheart's line.

Again, the talk ran to the unbelievable cost of some of the feasts the ancient Persian monarchs had been wont to give, and the wholesale quantity of priceless wines drunk at those banquets. Whereat. Cleopatra offered to wager that she could drink ten million sesterces ($450,000) worth of wine at a single sitting.

Antony loudly assured her that the thing was impossible. Even so redoubtable a tankard man as himself could not hope to drink one-hundredth that value of

wine in the most protracted debauch. She insisted.
The wager was made.

Calling for a goblet of "slaves' wine"—a species of
vinegar—the queen dropped into it the largest pearl
of Egypt's royal treasury, a gem appraised at four
hundred and fifty thousand dollars. The treasure dis-
solved under the vinegar's sharp acid; and Cleopatra
—to a gasp of horror from the more frugal onlookers—
drained the goblet.

Such banquets staggered Egypt's resources. So did
other jolly extravagances. Rumors of Antony's strange
infatuation reached Rome. Rome was used to Antony's love affairs, and Rome knew Cleopatra of
old.

So Rome merely grinned and shrugged its shoulders.
But when the big revenues that Antony had promised
to wring from the conquered country failed to arrive,
Rome—sorely wounded in the pocketbook—began to
protest.

Antony's friends at home pointed out to him what
capital the crafty Octavius would try to make of this
new-born dissatisfaction against his colleague. In a
momentary gleam of sanity, Antony left the weeping
Cleopatra and hastened back to Rome to face his
enemies.

There, all too briefly, the man's old genius flamed
up. He appeased the populace, won his former as-
cendency over the disapproving Senate, blocked Octavius' plot to hurl him from power, and sealed his

campaign of inspired diplomacy by marrying his rival's sister, Octavia.

At a stroke, Antony had won back all he had lost. Octavius was checkmated, the people were enthusiastic, and once more Antony had world rulership within his easy reach.

But in busy, iron-hard Rome, he fell to remembering the lazy sunshine of Egypt. The primly gentle Octavia was hopelessly insipid by contrast with the glowing super-woman. Memory tugged, ever harder and harder.

Even if this story were fiction, instead of prosy fact, you would foresee just what was bound to happen. Back to Egypt, on some flimsy pretext, fled Antony. He turned his back on Rome, on his wife, on Octavius, on friend, on foe, on future. He was to see none of them again. Nor was there to be a second outflash of his old genius. The rest was—Cleopatra.

The reunited lovers flew from bliss to bliss, from one mad extravagance to another. Statecraft, regal dignity—common sense—all went by the board.

At Rome, the effect of Antony's whirlwind reinstatement campaign gradually wore off. Revenues did not flow in from Egypt. But all sorts of wild stories did. And the wilder they were, the truer they were. Rome at large did not bother its brutal head over Antony's morals. But all Rome stormed and howled over the fact that the boundlessly rich kingdom of Egypt was bringing in practically no more money to the coffers of Rome. It was as if men who had invested a fortune in a thirty-story office building should find that the superintendent was holding back all the rents and losing tenants every day.

Octavius was quick to take advantage of all this. Personally, he hated Antony, and he was bitterly resentful of his sister's desertion. Politically, he wanted to be lord of the world—as later he was—under the title of "Emperor Augustus;" and poor, enfeebled Antony alone stood in his way.

On the plea that a new money-getter was needed for Rome in Antony's place, Octavius easily roused public feeling into a clamor that Egypt be invaded, Antony overthrown, and Cleopatra put to death. Octavius, as master of Rome, headed the punitive army of invasion.

Again, on news of his foes' approach, Antony's spirit—but this time not his genius—flickered back to a ghost of its old flame. By messenger, he sent Octavius a very sporting offer: namely, that waste of lives be avoided by Octavius and Antony meeting in single combat, to the death; "winner take all."

But Octavius was a politician, not a d'Artagnan; which is why he at last became Emperor of Rome and ruler of the known earth. He had not those cold, light eyes and thin lips for nothing. He was a strategist rather than a gladiator. Back to the challenger came this terse reply:

"Can Antony find no readier mode of death than at the sword of Octavius?"

On moved the invaders. And Antony took enough time from Cleopatra's side to make halfhearted preparations to resist. The first clash of any importance was the sea fight off Actium. There Fortune was inclined for the time to smile once again on her old prime favorite. All along the line, Antony's warships were driving back and breaking the formation of Octavius'. Then, at the crucial moment of the fight, Cleopatra, who, in a royal galley, was watching the conflict, ordered her galley put about and headed for the distant shore. To this day no one knows whether her fatal order was the result of a whim or of sudden cowardice or of both.

Her galley swept away from the battle. Antony, seeing it depart, feared Cleopatra might have been wounded by a stray arrow. At once he forgot that the issue of the day depended solely on him. He realized only that the woman he worshipped might be injured. And he ordered his own galley to put off in pursuit of Cleopatra's.

The captains of Antony's other ships, seeing their leader apparently running away, were seized with panic terror, and followed. The fight became a rout. Antony's fleet was annihilated.

With that strangely won battle, the last real obstacle between Octavius and complete victory was down. Steadily the conqueror advanced on Alexan-

dria. Cleopatra saw how things were going. She
knew that Antony was forever broken, and that, as
a protector against the oncoming Romans, he was
helpless. So she thriftily shifted her allegiance to
Octavius; sending him word that she was his admiring
slave, and that she craved a personal interview.

It was the same old siren trick. At sight, when she
was sixteen, she had won Cæsar's heart; at sight, when
she was twenty-eight, she had won Antony's heart
and soul. On sight, now, at thirty-eight, she hoped to
make of Octavius a second Antony. But Cæsar had
had black eyes, and Antony's eyes were a soft brown;
whereas the eyes of Octavius were pale gray and fire-
less. Had Cleopatra bothered to study physiognomy,
she might have sought some more hopeful plan than
to enslave such a man as this new invader.

Octavius, cold and heartless as he was, would not
trust himself to meet the super-woman; which was,
perhaps, the highest of the billion tributes that were,
soon or late, paid to Cleopatra's charms.

Instead, Octavius sent her a courteous message, assuring her of his respect and infinite admiration, and
saying that he would see that she was treated with
every consideration due her rank. To his friends,
however, he loudly boasted that she should walk barefoot through Rome, bound by gold chains to his chariot
axle. And word of this boast came to Cleopatra.
The game was up.

She walled herself into the huge Royal Mausoleum

and had word sent forth that she was dead. Antony, himself in hiding from the advancing Romans, heard and believed. Nothing was left. He had blithely thrown away the world for love. And now, after ten years of glorious happiness, the woman for whom he had been so glad to sacrifice everything, was dead.

His foes were hastening to seize him. There was but one course for a true Roman in such a plight to follow. The example of Brutus, of Cato, of a hundred other iron patriots, rose before him. And their example Antony followed.

He drove his sword through his body and fell dying, just as news came to him that Cleopatra lived. With almost his last breath, Antony ordered his slaves to carry him to the queen. The doors and lower windows of the mausoleum were bricked up. There was no time to send for masons to break an opening in them, if the dying man would reach Cleopatra alive. So he was lifted by ropes to an upper window of the tomb, and was then swung into the room where Cleopatra awaited him.

And in the arms of the woman who had wrecked him, and who at the last—though. mercifully, he never knew it—had sought to betray him, Mark Antony died. Perhaps it was an ignoble death, and an anticlimax. Perhaps it was a fit end for the life of this man, who had ever been the adored of women; and the death he himself would have chosen. Fate seldom makes a blunder in setting her scenes.

So perished Mark Antony; to whose life and death, before you judge him, I beg you to apply the words of a country preacher I once heard. The preacher was discanting on the Biblical personage "out of whom were cast seven devils."

"Brethren," said the exhorter, "a man must be far above the ordinary, to **contain** seven devils. In the average man's petty nature there isn't room even for a single half-size devil, to say nothing of seven full-grown ones."

Cleopatra had long since made up her mind to die sooner than walk in chains through the streets where once she had swept as Cæsar's peerless sweetheart. But she was part Greek and part Egyptian—both soft nations, lacking in the stern qualities of Rome. She had no taste for naked steel. She was content to die, but she wanted to die without pain.

On certain of her slaves she practiced the effects of various Oriental poisons. Some of these slaves died in agony, some in mere discomfort. One of them died with a smile on his lips—a slave on whom had been inflicted the bite of the tiny gray Nile-mud asp.

Cleopatra's question was answered. She put an asp to her breast. The serpent fixed its fangs in her white flesh.

And Cleopatra—model and synonym for a worldful of super-women—was very comfortably spared the shame of walking chained and barefoot in a Roman Triumph.

CHAPTER VIII.

GEORGE SAND

THE HOPELESSLY UGLY SIREN

A VERY famous woman discovered once that men are not paragons of fidelity. Or, finding that one man was not, she decided that all men were alike. And to Jules Sandeau, who had deceived her, she exclaimed, in fine, melodrama frenzy:

"My heart is a grave!"

"From the number of its occupants," drawled Sandeau, "I should rather call it a cemetery."

The woman, too angry to grasp the meaning of the ungallant speech, raged on:

"But I will be avenged. I shall write the tragedy of my love—in romance form—and—"

"Why not in city-directory form?" suggested the man.

And the loverly conversation ended in hysterics.

The woman was Amandine Lucile Aurore Dupin Dudevant. History, literature, and the annals of super-women know her as George Sand.

As one may glean from her verbal tilt with Sandeau,
she was not a recluse or a misanthropist.   In fact, she
numbered her ardent wooers by the dozen.   Her love
life began at a convent school when she was little more
than a child, and it endured until old age set in.   Perhaps a list of its victims, as Sandeau so cruelly hinted,
would have resembled a city directory.   It certainly
would have borne a striking likeness to a cyclopedic
index of Europe's nineteenth-century celebrities; for it
embraced such immortal names as De Musset, Sandeau,
Balzac, Chopin, Carlyle, Prosper Merimee, Liszt,
Dumas and many another.   So many demigods
knelt at her shrine that at last she wrote:

I am sick of great men.   I would far rather see them in
Plutarch than in real life. In Plutarch or in marble or in bronze,
their human side would not disgust me so.

And the personality, the appearance, the Venusberg
charm of this heart monopolist?   One instinctively
pictures a svelte form, a "face that launched a thousand ships," and all the rest of the sirenic paraphernalia
that instinctively attach themselves to one's mental
vision of a wholesale fracturer of hearts.   Here is
Balzac's description of her.   It is found in a letter
written to Madame Hanska in 1838, when George
Sand was at the acme of her super-woman career:

I found her in her dressing gown, smoking an after-dinner
cigar, beside the fire in an immense room.   She wore very

pretty yellow slippers with fringes, coquettish stockings, and red trousers. Physically, she has acquired a double chin, like a well-fed priest. She has not a single white hair, in spite of her terrible misfortunes. Her beautiful eyes are as sparkling as ever.

When she is sunk in thought, she looks just as stupid as formerly—as I told her— for her expression lies wholly in her eyes. She goes to bed at six in the morning and rises at noon. (I go to bed at six in the evening and rise at midnight; but, of course, I am conforming myself to her habits.) She smokes to excess and plays, perhaps, too much the grande dame.

Carlyle, still less merciful, snarls forth the following wholly Carlylean epitome of George Sand's looks:

"She has the face of a horse!"

Another contemporary writer declares:

"Her hair is as black and shiny as ebony; her swarthy face is red and heavy; her expression fierce and defiant, yet dull."

So much for the verity of traditional siren dreams! So much, too, for the theory that beauty or daintiness or feminity has anything to do with the nameless charm of the world's super-women.

George Sand came, honestly, if lefthandedly, by her cardiac prowess. For she was a great-great-grand-daughter of Adrienne Lecouvreur and Marshal Saxe; two of history's stellar heart breakers—a fact of which she made much.

Her father was a French army officer—Lieutenant Dupin—and as a mere baby his only daughter, Aurore, was acclaimed "daughter of the regiment." Decked out in a tiny uniform, the ugly duckling ran wild in the army posts where her father was stationed, and joined right boisterously in the soldiers' rough sports.

Later, she was sent to a convent. From her own description of this particular retreat, it was a place that crushed out all normal and childish ideas and filled the growing mind with a morbid melancholy. Yet it was there that love first found the girl.

The victim—or victor—was one Stephane de Grandsaigne, professor of physiology. Under his tuition she developed a queer craving for dissection—a fad she followed, in psychic form, through life. The love scenes between herself and her adored professor were usually enacted while they were together dissecting a leg or an arm or probing the mysteries of retina and cornea.

It was a semigruesome, unromantic episode, and it ended with suddenness when the pupil was sent out into the world. There a husband was found for her. He was Casimer Dudevant, a man she liked well enough and who was mildly fond of her. They lived together for a time in modified content. Two children were born to them.

By and by, Casimir took to drink. Many people refused to blame him. Indeed, there are present-day students of George Sand's life who can find a host of excuses for his bibulous failings. But once, coming home from a spree, Casimir forgot to take his wife's lofty reproaches with his wonted good nature.

In a flash of drunken anger, he struck her. And she left him.

The high spirit of her act of independence is marred just a little by the fact that she chanced to be in love with another man. This other man was Aurelian de Seze, a ponderous country magistrate. The affair was brief. Presently the two had parted. And George Sand, penniless, went to Paris to make a living by literature.

She obtained hack work of a sort, lived in the typical drafty garret so dear to unrecognized genius, and earned for a time only fifteen francs—three dollars— a month. It was the customary nadir, wherein one gathers equipment for success.

Then she met Jules Sandeau. He was a lawyer who dabbled in literature. He fell in love with the lonely woman and she with him. They formed a literary partnership. Together they wrote novels and began to achieve a certain measure of good luck. Their novels were signed "George Sand." Why. no one knows. It was a pen name devised by the feminine member of the novelistic firm.

But before long Sandeau was left far behind in the race for fame. His more or less fair partner wrote a novel on her own account. It was "Indiana." Like Byron, she woke one morning to find herself famous. The book had lifted her forever out of obscurity and need.

At about the same period, she entered Sandeau's

study one day just in time to see him kiss another woman. The other woman chanced to be their laundress, who, presumably, was more kissable, if less inspiring, than was the newly acclaimed celebrity on whom Sandeau had been lavishing his fickle affections.

There was a scene, unequaled for violence in any of their joint novels. And in the course of it occurred the repartee recorded at the beginning of this story. As an upshot, Sandeau followed Dudevant, de Seze, Grandsaigne, and the rest into the limbo of George Sand's discarded lovers; where he was soon to be joined by many another and far greater man.

Her faith in men shattered for at lest the fourth time, George Sand forswore fidelity and resolved to make others suffer; even as she liked to imagine she herself had suffered. The literary world was by this time cheering itself hoarse over her. And literary giants were vying for her love.

Out of the swarm, she selected Prosper Merimee. The author of "Carmen" was then in his prime as a lion of the salons. To him George Sand gave her heart irrevocably and forever. Through youth and maturity they worshiped each other—for eight consecutive days. On the ninth day, George Sand informed "Carmen's" creator that he was far too cynical to be her ideal any longer. Merimee retorted that her "pose of divine exaltation" was better suited to an angel than to an ugly woman who continually smoked cigars and who swore as pyrotechnically as one of her

father's most loquacious troopers.   So the romance
ended.

Followed a bevy of loves well-nigh as brief, most
of whose heroes' names are emblazoned on the book
backs of the world's libraries.   And after this populous
interregnum, came Alfred de Musset.

De Musset was a mere boy.   But his wonderful
poetry had already awakened Europe to ecstacy.   He
was the beau-ideal of a million youthful lovers and
their sweethearts; even as, a generation earlier, Byron
had been.

It was in 1833 that he and George Sand met.   De
Musset had seen her from afar and had begged for
an introduction.   She was six years older than he, and
the prettiest girls in France were pleading wistfully for
his smile.   But, at sight, he loved the horse-faced,
almost middle-aged swearer of strange oaths and
smoker of strong cigars.   Hence his plea to be introduced.

Sainte-Beuve, to whom he made the request, wrote,
asking leave to bring him to one of George Sand's "at
homes."   The same day she returned a most positive
refusal, writing:

> I do not want you to introduce De Musset to me.   He is a
> fop, and we would not suit each other.   Instead, bring Dumas;
> in whose art I have found a soul, if only the soul of a com-
> mercial traveler.

But de Musset, unrebuffed, succeeded in his ambition. He managed to secure an introduction to her at a banquet given by the **Revue des Deux Mondes** editors. And almost at once his love was reciprocated. Then began a union that was alternately the interest, the scandal, and the laughing-stock of a continent.

Each of the lovers was a genius; each had been pedestaled by the world; each was supposed to live on a rarified plane far above the heads or the ken of mere earth folk. The love affair of two such immortals might reasonably be expected—**was** expected—to be akin to the noble romances of poetry.

As a matter of fact, its three-year course was one long series of babyish spats, of ridiculous scenes, and of behavior worthier the inmates of a mad-house or a kindergarten than of the decade's two master intellects.

George Sand expected De Musset to live on the heights of bloodless idealism. When he did so, she berated him as heartless. When he failed to, she denounced him as an animal. She was never content with whatever course he might follow. Yet she was madly in love with him.

During their brief separations, she avalanched him with letters; some furious, some imploring, some wildly affectionate, some drearily commonplace. Here is an extract from one, displaying a fair sample of her warmer moods:

It is nothing to you to have tamed the pride of such a woman as I, and to have stretched me a suppliant at your feet?

It is nothing to you that I am dying of love?—torment of my life that you are!

In the course of the cranky affair they journeyed to Italy. There, in turn, both fell ill. And there, through the medium of the sick room, both met a handsome young Italian doctor, Pietro Pagello. He, like so many others before and after him, fell victim to George Sand's mysterious charm.

Pagello's dark good looks, and his vivacity temporarily swept George Sand's heart far out of poor convalescent de Musset's reach. She became blindly infatuated with the young doctor. De Musset, jealously sick and sickly jealous, was quick to see how matters stood. And with true Gallic sensationalism, he rose to the dramatic occasion.

First he swore eternal brotherhood and loyalty to the doctor—whom he scarcely knew—and then, joining the embarrassed Pagello's hand to George Sand's, the poet tearfully declaimed:

"I know all. You love each other. Take him, Aurore, as the parting gift of a lover you have ceased to love. Take her, Pietro, as a memento of your sworn friend. Adieu, both of you—forever!"

De Musset strode forth from the room in a style that would have evoked an applause storm from even a deaf-and-dumb gallery. He left Italy and came back to France. There he loudly bewailed his fate and moaned rhythmically anent the false flame of woman's love.

Meanwhile, George Sand found to her surprise that she loved the dramatic de Musset far more than she loved Pagello. She followed de Musset to Paris, bringing Pagello along for good measure.

When she had gone to Italy with de Musset, Paris had gasped. Even the usual latitude allowed to geniuses had been perilously stretched. When de Musset had returned, Orpheuslike, weeping all over the strings of his lyre, Paris had wept with him. But now that the heroine of the escapade followed in full chase of the discarded one, dragging his successor in her wake, Paris howled with inextinguishable laughter.

De Musset, poetically sensitive to every change of opinion, refused to make himself ridiculous. While renewing his vow of brotherly friendship for Pagello, he utterly refused to see George Sand, or to answer one of her thousand beseeching letters.

Pagello, too, began to feel supremely uncomfortable in his thankless role of excess baggage. He squirmed nervously in search of a door of escape. He quickly found one.

"Monsieur de Musset must hate me for what I have done," he announced to all who would stop laughing long enough to listen to him. "He has probably sworn a blood feud against me. I will not remain here to become the victim of a vendetta."

And he fled incontinently to his native Italy, leaving George Sand alone to face the now redoubled spasms of public mirth.

Tragically humorless, deaf to snicker and guffaw, she set herself to the tedious task of winning back de Musset. When letters were of no avail, she sought to waylay him in the street or elsewhere. Forewarned, he kept to his rooms.

Then she stationed herself on his doorstep and wept there, like a modern and uglier Niobe, for all to see. De Musset kept still closer hidden from view.

In desperation, the unhappy woman resolved to follow the historic example of Ninon de Lenclos in reclaiming an errant lover. She cut off her heavy black hair—her one beauty—and sent it by messenger to the coy de Musset.

The sacrifice was vain. Perhaps the beauty-loving poet, remembering how homely she had looked, even with her luxuriant hair, drew a vivid mind picture of what she must look like without it. At all events, he made no sign of forgiveness.

One day, de Musset, coming unguardedly out of his apartment, collided on the stairs with the weeping woman. There was a partial and very temporary reconciliation, followed soon by a permanent break.

George Sand, tingling with hurt pride, proceeded to write a novel, wherein, under a painfully thin and openwork veil, she told the story of her love affair with de Musset. It is waste of space to add that she told it from her own angle, depicting herself as a gentle, too-loving martyr, and painting de Musset as a false, affected, ludicrously worthless personage.

The novel set Paris to jabbering as noisily as it had just laughed. De Musset was regarded as a monster, a monument of duplicity, and his former sweetheart as a patient saint. But the poet was not long in preparing a counterblast.

Promptly he threw into the arena a book in which, under still thinner disguise, he gave his own version of the story. In this volume de Musset was a trusting lover, and George Sand a viper.

There were further recriminations, in print and out of it. Literary Paris was divided into two camps. Between the pro-Mussets and the pro-Sands, the war raged merrily. Swinburne crystalized the case in a deathless epigram:

"De Musset was wrong; but George did **not** behave as a gentleman should."

For a time, George Sand turned to her work for oblivion. She wrote eight hours a day. Her novels were among the foremost of the century. She was France's best-known woman. The men who had loved her served now as characters for her books, as had de Musset. Mercilessly she dissected them—memories of the physiology professor!—and held up to scorn their faults, their frailties, their crass humanness. There was gnashing of teeth. There was recognition—wholesale. There was protest. There were legions of threats to prosecute. Said merry old Abbe Liszt—himself a heart conqueror of renown:

"Each of your admirers, madame, is a butterfly

which you lure to you by honey, impale upon the pin of jealously or boredom, and finally vivisect in a novel."

After a mere breathing space came what was probably the grand passion of George Sand's ultra-passionate life; a romance with none of the ironic humor that lighted her affair with De Musset.

The hero—victim—what you will—was Frederic Chopin; too-fiery soul in too-fragile body. Genius, wonder musician, dreamer, the man had always been tossed on misfortune's waters. hammered by them till his mighty soul had well-nigh torn free from the failing flesh. And at this period, of all others, fate threw him into the life of George Sand.

He was slender, weak, almost effeminate in his unfleshliness. She was brutally robust, mannish, aggressive; his exact opposite· And they loved—loved more deeply, more all-absorbingly than either had loved before in a mutually long era of heart destroying. In fact, George Sand loved Chopin as she loved nothing else on earth—with the sole exception of her idolized self.

The hand of death was already on Chopin when he and George Sand met. This supervital woman seemed to breathe into him some of her own tireless vitality. His health rallied. It was said by fanciful acquaintances that George Sand's life was keeping life in her lover. She heard and was glad, and hastened to proclaim the wonder to her friends, adding thereby a leaf to her martyr crown. By sheer will power and excess vital force she actually buoyed up her frail lover's sinking strength and gave him a new lease of living.

This did not prevent her from quarreling fiercely and frequently with him—as she always did with every man or woman who came into personal acquaintance with her.

Chopin begged her to marry him. She refused. One venture in matrimony had sufficed her. Not even to make happy the man she loved would she essay a second trial of wedlock.

In her first onrush of devotion for Chopin she could not blind herself to the fact that, even as she had tired of others, so she might one day tire of him. And divorces in France, were not easy to get. Hence, the dying Chopin's supreme wish went ungratified; as had many a lesser wish during his affair with her.

The sick composer had known many loves. Yet from the hour he met George Sand he seems to have been steadfast to that single devotion. It is not on record that he so much as aroused her ever-wakeful jealousy. And he is probably the only man of her love-starred career who did not—which is odd, in view of this assertion by one of Chopin's biographers:

He found himself unable to avoid accepting some of the numberless hearts that were flung like roses at his feet. He could modulate from one love affair to another as fleetly and as gracefully as from one key to its remote neighbor.

Here, too, is the account given by a later chronicler of the composer's meeting with George Sand:

One evening, as he was entering a house where a literary reception was in progress, Chopin fancied he was pursued by a violet-scented phantom. In superstitious fear, he would have left the house at once, but friends who were with him laughed away his dread and described the phenomenon as the fancy of a sick man's brain.

He entered the crowded salon and was forthwith presented to the guest of honor, a swarthy and strange-looking woman—the premiere novelist, Madame Dudevant—George Sand.

In his diary that same night Chopin wrote of his new acquaintance:

I do not like her face. There is something in it that repels me.

Yet within a day or so he was her adorer.

For a time all went as well as any love story could with such a heroine. She gloried in her power to build up for the moment her lover's waning strength. Her friends' praise of the feat was as music to her. But she was not the type of woman who can forever wait patiently upon a fretful convalescent's whims. Her self-sacrifice was a flash, not a steady flame.

And in time she girded at the restraints of playing nurse and vitality giver. Then, instead of boasting as before, she waxed complaining. She told the world at large how exacting and cross and tiresome Chopin was.

She once referred to him publicly as "that detestable invalid." She announced that she was his ever-patient comrade and nurse. There is no authority but hers to bear out the claim of patience. And so the once-beautiful relationship dragged out its weary length until George Sand could endure the strain no longer.

She deserted Chopin.

Not content with this final blow to the invalid who had loved her for years, she continued to vilify him. Among her complaints was one that has since passed, in slightly altered form, into a good old reliable vaudeville wheeze. She wrote:

> We never addressed a single reproach to each other except once. And that was from the first to the last time we met.

George Sand's desertion was Chopin's deathblow. He never rallied from it. He tried to mask his heartbreak by going about as before and appearing often in public. But even this was soon denied to him— not only by collapsed health, but from the danger of meeting his former divinity at the houses he chanced to visit or on the streets. One such lesson was enough for him. It was in a friend's crowded drawing-room. A historian describes the encounter:

> Thinking herself unobserved, George Sand walked up to Chopin and held out her hand.
>
> "Frederic!" she murmured, in a voice audible to him alone.
>
> He saw her familiar form standing before him. She was repentant, subdued, and seeking reconciliation. His handsome face grew deadly pale, and without a word he left the room.

The end came soon afterward. Chopin's mortal illness struck him down. Dying, he sent for his lost love. Perhaps the message never reached her; perhaps she thought it a trick—she had tried something of the sort on de Musset; perhaps she did not realize that the time was so short.

At all events, she paid no heed to the frantic appeal that she come at once to the dying composer.

Hour after hour, Chopin waited for her, his ears strained for the sound of her heavy tread. At last he grew to realize that she would not obey the summons, that he would never again see her.

As hope fled, Chopin broke down and cried piteously.

"She promised I should die in no arms but hers!" he sobbed over and over.

And that night he died—no less than seven different women claiming later to have taken his recreant sweetheart's place at his deathbed.

George Sand was conscience-stricken. She wrote and proclaimed long and more or less plausible reasons to account for her failure to go to Chopin. But no one who really knew her was convinced of her excuses' truth. And so ended one more of her heart stories.

De Musset, by the way refused to admit her to his rooms when he himself lay dying—a grisly joke that Paris appreciated.

Back to her work, as once before, George Sand fled for forgetfulness. And her fame grew. She was the most prolific woman writer, by the way, in literature's history; writing, in all, twenty plays and more than one hundred novels.

An Englishman (name buried) courted her at about this time. Still miserable over Chopin's death —and far more so over the way people were talking about her treatment of him—she was decidedly waspish to the trans-Channel admirer. Seeking to win her interest, in a literary discussion, he opened one conversation by inquiring:

"Madame Dudevant, what is your favorite novel?"

"Olympia,'" she answered, without a second of hesitance.

"'Olympia?'" the Englishman repeated, vainly ransacking his memory. "I don't think I recall any book of that name."

"Of course you don't," she snapped. "I haven't written it yet."

And perhaps—or perhaps not—his British brain some day unraveled the meaning of cryptic retort.

For her infidelities George Sand felt no compunction. She wrote frankly concerning them:

I have never imposed constancy upon myself. When I have felt that love is dead, I have said so without shame or remorse, and have obeyed Providence that was leading me elsewhere.

By her marriage with Dudevant, she had had a son and a daughter. The daughter, Solange, inherited much of her mother's lawlessness, with none of the latter's inspiration. And now George Sand was to see how her own nature worked in another of the same blood.

She arranged a splendid marriage for Solange, a marriage with a man of rank and money. And on the very eve of the wedding Solange proceeded to elope with a poor sculptor, Clesinger by name.

The mother was equal to the emergency. She ran after the fugitives, caught them, bullied Clesinger into marrying Solange, hushed all scandal, and installed the young couple in a Paris flat, settling on them the bulk of her property. In revenge, Clesinger permanently estranged Solange from her mother.

Soon afterward George Sand's sway over men's hearts ceased. Whether she was weary of love, or whether love was weary of her, the old fascination deserted her. No more as lovers, but as profound admirers of her intellect, great men still flocked about her—Matthew Arnold, Flaubert, Feuillet, and a host of others. But it was now her brain alone they worshiped.

By many years George Sand outlived her charm, dying in 1876 at the age of seventy-two, her grandchildren about her—a smugly proper, if sadly anticlimactic, ending to a career in which anticlimax had been almost as infrequent as propriety.

CHAPTER NINE.

MADAME DU BARRY

THE SEVEN-MILLION-DOLLAR SIREN.

S HE came from the same neighborhood that had
produced Joan of Arc. She even claimed relationship to the long-dead Maid. But at that point
all likeness between the two comes to a very abrupt
end.

She is known to history as "Marie Jeanne Gomard
de Vaubernier, Comtesse du Barry." The parish register of her birthplace describes her, less flamboyantly,
as "Marie Jeanne, natural daughter of Anne Becu,
known as Quantigny; born Aug., A. D. 1746."

There are many details in Marie Jeanne du Barry's
story that I am going to omit—at my own request; not
only because they are unwriteable, but because their
sordid vulgarity is also drearily stupid. I apologize in
advance for the omissions. But even after the pro-
cess of weeding out, I think there will be quite enough
left to hold the interest.

When Marie was six, Anne Becu drifted to Paris—

the Mecca of her trade. And soon afterward, an admirer of Anne's, one Dumonceau, was coaxed into lavishing two dollars and forty cents a month on Marie's education. Dumonceau had been one of Anne's wooers in the village days, and it has been suggested that his interest in little Marie was prompted by more than mere kindness—in fact, that he and the infant were "more than kin and less than kind."

In any case, the monthly two dollars and forty cents paid Marie's expenses in a convent school, where she spent the next ten years. This Sainte-Aurore convent, in the Rue Neuve Sainte-Genevieve, was a philanthropic refuge "for all young persons of honest parentage who are in circumstances where they run the risk of ruin."

The rules of the Sainte-Aurore were far stricter and icier than those of the most investigatable of modern orphanages. Among the punishments inflicted on these little wards of God were starvation, beatings, and imprisonment in cold and stone-floored dark cells— for the very mildest transgressions.

Three dire sins, calling always for instant retribution, were: "To laugh, to sing, and to speak above a whisper." For such hideous and unnatural crimes as laughter, song, and ordinary speech, these poor loveless babies were treated like the vilest criminals. One hopes, morbidly, that the theologians who abolished Hell left at least one warm corner of it in commission, for the framers and enforcers of those gentle rules.

All the foregoing is not sentimental mush, but is mentioned to show how dire must have been a pupil's sin that the convent authorities could not cope with.

And such a sin—no one knows what it was—Marie committed when she was sixteen. For which she was expelled in black disgrace from her happy childhood home at Sainte-Aurore, and turned loose upon the world.

Her mother's loving arms were open, ready to receive and succor the disgraced girl, and to start her afresh in life—as only a mother can. So, to keep Marie from feeling unduly dependent upon a poor working woman like herself, she taught her her own trade—the oldest on earth.

With a little basket of cheap jewelry—which served the same purpose as a present-day beggar's stock of lead pencils—Marie went the rounds of the streets. Her career was cut out for her by her mother's fond forethought. And in nine hundred and ninety-nine cases out of a thousand, a girl thus launched would have ended in the gutter. But Marie was the thousandth woman—a true super-woman, in every sense of the word. The filth of the streets could not smirch her—outwardly. And luck was waiting around the corner for her.

A rich and eccentric old woman of fashion—Madame Legrade—had a craze for amateur theatricals. Catching sight of Marie one day, she was struck by the girl's beauty, and hired her, partly as a companion and partly as a comedian for her private theatre.

At Madame Legrade's, Marie got her first view of semidecent society. And, being adaptable, she picked up a smatttering of manners and of grammatical speech; only a smattering, but all she cared to acquire. There, too, she met such men as the withered old wit, de Richelieu, and the Prince de Soubise; and the Duc de Brissac, whose son was one day to be the one real love of her life. Here, too, she met a genius whom she describes in her "Memoirs" as "a cunning fox; witty . . . very ugly and very thin." He was Grimm, the fairytale man.

Marie was in clover. But the fortune was too good to last. And because a far more glittering fortune was awaiting her just around the corner, Destiny soon joggled the girl out of her snug berth. Madame Legrade had two sons. Both of them fell crazily in love with Marie. It is not on record that she told them she would rather be the poor working girl that she was. And Madame Legrade, in horror, ordered her out of the house.

Back to her dear, old loving mother, as before, went Marie. And once more mother love came to the rescue. Anne Becu had recently married a lackey of some great house. She was now "Madame Racon." Marie adopted her stepfather's name—the first to which she had ever possessed even a semilegal claim—and permitted her mother to get her a job in the millinery shop of Madame Labille. This shop was of a sort extremely common in that day. It sold not only hats for woman, but sword knots and shoe buckles for men. It employed only girls of extreme beauty. And it was a favorite louging place for men about town. Altogether, there was no startling change in Marie's vocation from the era when she had hawked artificial jewelry.

Her presence drew scores of young dandies to the shop. And she might readily have had her pick of the lot. But during a momentary weakness of intellect, she plunged into a love affair with a handsome young pastry cook, Nicolas Mothon. The other and more ambitious girls guyed her right unmercifully for her plebeian tastes. But it was terribly serious with Marie. Mathon was the first man to whom she had lost her heart. Many years later she wrote:

When I call to memory all the men who have adored me, I must say it was not poor Nicolas who pleased me least. For I, too, have known what first love can mean.

But she forgot what "first love can mean" as readily as she had learned it. For soon she threw over Nicolas for a man of wealth, named De la Vauvenardiere; and she abandoned the latter for a suitor named Duval; and ousted Duval from her affection for Lamet, the court hairdresser.

No, in choosing Lamet, she was not lowering her standard. A court hairdresser was far more than a

mere barber. He was a functionary of vast importance, the confidant of the great, the counselor of the
unwary, a man of substance and position, the only
tradesman in all France who was permitted by court
edict to wear a sword.

Marie was envied as Lamet's sweetheart; until he
went broke, overnight, and had to flee to England to
dodge a debtor's cell.

Then came the Cosse incident; at least, then it began. Cosse—or Louis Hercule Timoleon de Cosse-
Brissac—was the Duc de Brissac's son. He met Marie
in the street one day, so runs the story, followed her to
the shop, and there, under the pretext of buying a
sword knot, fell into talk with her. He loved her at
first sight, and she loved him. Theirs was not such a
love as either had hitherto known. It was the genuine
article.

Cosse was young and good looking and afflicted with
republican ideas. He did not see in Marie the vender
of cheap jewelry and cheaper affections, nor the girl
who used her millinery job as a mask. To him, she was
an angel. And—so far as concerned him—she was.

They were young, and they dreamed. Cosse was
unlike any man Marie had known. His love was utterly unlike any love she had known or heard of. Altogether, it was a pretty little romance, on both sides.
And if we smile at it, let the smile be kindly, with
nothing of the leer about it. For there was nothing
to provoke a leer—at least, not then.

This Cosse affair's early stages are so intertangled with romance, legend, court rumor, and later inventions, that I hasten to forestall corrections, from readers wiser than I, by confessing that all I know of it, or can learn from supposedly reliable sources, is that Marie and Cosse parted somewhat suddenly; and the causes variously given are that his father put a stop to the romance and that Cosse learned something of Marie's real character. It is gravely declared that he wanted to marry her, and that his indignant ducal parent not only opened his eyes to the bride elect's past, but threatened to throw Cosse into the Bastille by means of a **lettre de cachet.** As I said, I vouch for none of these reasons for the break between the two lovers. It is all surmise. But what follows is not.

The next man to lose his head and heart to Marie was a young nobleman whose repute may be guessed from the fact that—even in dissolute eighteenth-century Paris—he was known, not as a roue, but as **"The Roue."** He had come to Paris a few years earlier, leaving a wife somewhere on the way.

He had squandered his patrimony en route, and reached the capital penniless. But he quickly caught the fancy of Madame Malouse, who had influence at court. She arranged that he should have practically the sole monopoly of supplying the French navy with all its various forms of merchandise. This meant fat profits, and he fattened them still further by running a select gambling house.

He was Jean, Vicomte du Barry.

Jean met and fell victim to Marie. Realizing what a cash attraction her beauty and charm could be made, he installed her as presiding genius of his gambling house, as a lure to draw youthful nobles to the place. Marie—or Madame Lange, as, for no known reason, she had begun to call herself—was the bright star at the Chance Goddess' shrine. And the money poured fast into the crooked games whereby the house made Jean rich.

For a time there was wholesale prosperity all around, with plenty more of it to come. Before I go on, may I quote a contemporary writer's word picture of Marie, as she appeared at this time?

> Her hair is long, silky, curling like a child's, and blond with a natural ash tint. . . . Her eyebrows and lashes are dark and curly. Behind them the blue eyes, which one seldom sees quite open, look out with coquettish, sidelong glances. . . . Her nose is small and finely cut, and her mouth is a perfect cupid's bow. . . . Her neck, her arms, and her feet and hands remind one of ancient Greek statuary; while her complexion is that of a rose leaf steeped in milk. . . . She carries with her a delicious atmosphere of intoxication, victorious, amorous youth.

Voltaire once exclaimed, before a portrait of her: "The original was made for the gods!"

Even as the cherry tree was posthumously invented for Washington and, perhaps, the apple for William

Tell and the egg for Columbus, so around Marie in after years sprang up countless tales of her youth. Some may have been true. Some were palpable lies. To which does the ensuing anecdote belong?

In the spring of 1768, during her sojourn as "come-on" for the du Barry gambling hell, Marie noticed, three days in succession, that she was closely followed on the street by "a young man of a sober cast of countenance and elegant attire." Now, to be followed was no novelty to Marie. And more than one man of "elegant attire" had sued in vain for her favor. Yet this youth made no advances. He simply followed her wherever she went. And in his absence his face haunted her strangely. So, on the fourth day, as she turned suddenly in the street and saw him close behind her, she asked, with affected indignation:

"What do you want of me?"

The man bowed low, with no shadow of hesitancy, made this cryptic answer to her query:

"Mademoiselle, will you grant me the first reasonable request I may make of you when you are Queen of France?"

Thinking he was a crank—as perhaps he was—she sought to humor him, and replied:

"Certainly, monsieur. I promise."

"You take me for a madman," he returned, with a second grave bow. "But I am not insane. Adieu, mademoiselle. There will be nothing more extraordinary than your elevation—except your end."

He spoke and vanished, either into the street crowd
or into thin air.

You may recall the story of the "Man in Black's"
midnight visit to Ninon de l'Enclos, with a gift to the
essence of youth and the warning of her death?   This
was a well-believed and oft-repeated narrative in
Marie's day.   It is highly possible that she built from it
her recital of the adventure of the "elegantly attired"
stranger.

At all events, she told Jean du Barry about it.
Whether or not he believed it, is no concern of yours or
mine.   But it assuredly gave him an idea; the supreme
idea of his rotten life.   He saw a one-in-fifty chance of
making more money through Marie than she could
have earned for him in a century as divinity of his
gambling rooms.   And, remote as were the scheme's
prospects for success, he resolved to make a gambler's
cast at the venture.

Louis XV., King of France, had been ruled for
nearly twenty years by the Marquise de Pompadour,
who had squandered royal revenues, had made and
unmade men's career by a nod or a shake of her pretty
head, and had played at ducks and drakes with international politics.   And now Madame de Pompadour
was dead.   Many a younger and prettier face had
caught Louis' doddering fancy, since her death.   But
no other **maitresse en titre** had ruled him and France
since then.

Briefly, Jean coveted the vacant office for Marie.

Not for her own sake. Jean did not care for her happiness or welfare, or for the happiness or welfare of any mortal on earth except of one Jean. Vicomte du Barry. But he foresaw that with Marie as the royal favorite, he himself, as her sponsor, could reap a harvest such as is not the guerdon of one man in a million.

He set to work at his self-appointed task with the same rare vigor and cunning that had so long enabled him to elude the hangman and to live on better men's money. The first step was to engage the help of Lebel, the king's **valet de chambre.**

Lebel was nominally a servant, but, in a sense, he was mightier than any prime minister. For Louis relied implicitly on the valet's taste in feminine beauty. It was Lebel, for instance, who had first brought Madame de Pompadour to the king's notice. He had done the same good turn to many another aspiring damsel. And now, heavily bribed by Jean du Barry, he consented to see if Marie was worth mentioning to Louis.

At sight of Marie, the connoisseur valet realized to the full her super-woman charm. He recognized her as the thousandth woman—even the millionth.

Yet Lebel was ever cautious about raising false hopes. So, not knowing that Jean had gone over the whole plan with Marie, he asked her if she would honor him by attending a little informal dinner he was soon to give, in his apartment, at the Versailles palace; a dinner in honor of "the Baron de Gonesse."

Marie, with sweet innocence, accepted the invitation; then timidly asked Lebel if she might sit beside him at the dinner, as all the others would be strangers to her. The bare thought of his presuming to sit down in the presence of the king—otherwise "the Baron de Gonesse"—so filled Lebel with horror that he forgot his role of diplomacy and blurted out:

"I? Sit at the table with **him**? I—I shall be unexpectedly called from the room, as usual, just as dinner is served. And I shall not return until it is over."

When Marie—carefully coached as to behavior, repartee, and so forth, by the ever-thoughtful Jean—arrived at Lebel's apartments in the palace. on the night of the dinner, she found, to her disgust, that the king was nowhere in sight—not even disguised as "the Baron de Gonesse"—and that her fellow guests were merely a group of Versailles officials.

Not being versed in palace secrets, she did not know that Louis was seated in a dark closet behind a film-curtained window, looking into the brightly lighted dining room and noting everything that went on, nor that cunningly arranged speaking tubes brought every whispered or loud-spoken word to him.

Finding the king was not to be one of the guests, the girl philosophically choked back her chagrin and set herself to get every atom of fun out of the evening that she could. She ate much, drank more, and behaved pretty much like a gloriously lovely street gamin. There was no use in wasting on these understrappers the fine speeches and the courtesy she had been learning for the king's benefit. So she let herself go. And the dinner was lively, to say the very least. In fact, it was the gayest, most deliciously amusing dinner ever held in those sedate rooms—thanks to Marie.

Louis, in paroxysms of laughter, looked on until the sound of his guffaws betrayed his royal presence. Then he came out of hiding.

Marie, for an instant, was thunder-struck at what she had done. She feared she had ruined her chances by the boisterous gayety of the past hour or so. Then —for her brain was as quick as her talk was dull— she saw the fight was not lost, but won, and she knew how she had won it.

Louis XV. was fifty-eight years old. He lived in France's most artificial period. No one dared be natural; least of all in the presence of the king. All his life he had been treated to honeyed words, profound reverence, the most polished and adroit courtesy. People—women especially—had never dared be human when he was around.

Marie saw that it was the novelty of her behavior which had aroused the king's bored interest. And from that moment her course was taken. She did not cringe at his feet, or pretend innocence, or assume **grande-dame** airs. She was **herself,** Marie Becu, the slangy, light-hearted, feather-brained daughter of the streets; respecting nothing, fearing nothing, confused by nothing—as ready to shriek gutter oaths at her king as at her footman. And, of course, she was also Marie

Becu, the super-woman whose magnetism and beauty were utterly irresistible.

The combination was too much for Louis. He succumbed. What else was there for him to do? After the myriad poses of the women he had known, Marie's naturalness was like a bracing breeze sweeping through a hothouse; a slum breeze, if you like, but none the less a breeze, and delightfully welcome to the jaded old monarch.

Louis fell in love with Marie. It was not a mere infatuation of an hour, like most of his affairs. He fell completely and foolishly in love with her. And he never fell out of love with her as long as he lived.

Lebel was in despair. He had hoped Marie might amuse the king. He had had no shadow of an idea that the affair would go further. By reason of his privileges as an old servant, he actually ventured to remonstrate with Louis.

"Sire," he protested, "she is not even legitimate. The birth records attest that."

"Then," laughed the king, "let the right authorities make her so."

Accordingly, messengers were sent posthaste to her babyhood home, and a new birth certificate was drawn up; also a certificate attesting to her mother's legal marriage to a wholly mythical Monsieur de Gomard de Vaubernier and to several other statements that made Marie's legitimacy as solid as Gibraltar.

"Also," pleaded the valet, "she is neither a wife nor a woman of title."

"We can arrange both those trifles," the king assured him.

And, with charming simplicity, the thing was done. Jean sent for his worthless elder brother, Guillaume, Comte du Barry, who was at that time an army captain. And on September 1, 1768, Marie and Guillaume were duly married. The lucky bridgegroom received enough money to pay all his debts and to make him rich. Then he obligingly deserted his new-made wife at the church door, according to program, and wandered away to spend his fortune as might best please him. Thereby, Marie Becu became Madame la Comtesse du Barry, without having her cur of a husband to bother about.

A list of her possessions and their values—duly set down in the marriage contract, which is still on file—shows the state of Marie's finances at this time. I copy it for the benefit of those who may be interested to learn of a useful life's by-products. At twenty-two—in 1768—so says the contract, Marie was the sole owner of:

One diamond necklace, worth sixteen hundred dollars; an aigret and a pair of earings in clusters, worth sixteen hundred dollars; thirty dresses and petticoats, worth six hundred dollars; lace, dress trimmings, caps, et cetera, worth twelve hundred dollars; six dozen shirts of fine linen, twelve complete morning

dresses, and other articles of linen, et cetera, worth four hundred dollars.

One obstacle alone now barred Marie's road to
supremacy. According to unbreakable royal etiquette,
three things were indispensable to the woman who
aspired to become a French king's **maitresse en titre**—
she must be legitimate, she must be of noble rank, and
she must have been presented at court.

The first two conditions, Marie had fulfilled. The
third was a poser. In order to be presented at court,
some reputable woman of the old nobility must act
as sponsor. And not one decent woman of high rank
would sink to acting as sponsor for Marie. Moreover,
the king declared he did not care whether she were
presented or not, and he would take no step to help
her in the matter.

Without this presentation, she could not appear publicly at court, she could not sway overt political influence, she could not have a suite of rooms at the
palace. Between a presentation and no presentation
lay all the difference between uncrowned queen and
a light o' love. And no one would sponsor Marie.

Jean du Barry, at last, solved the problem, as he
had solved all the rest.

He had able assistance. For, a court clique had been
formed to back Marie's pretensions. The clique was
headed by such men as the old Duc de Richelieu and
the much younger Duc d'Aiguillon. The latter was

violently in love with Marie, and there is no reason to think that his love was hopeless. But the rest of the clique cared not a straw about her. To them, the whole thing was a master move in politics. With Marie in control of the king, and themselves in control of Marie, they foresaw an era of unlimited power.

The Duc de Choiseul, prime minister of France, was the sworn enemy of this clique, which formed the "opposition." And Choiseul swore to move heaven and earth to prevent Marie's presentation, for he knew it would lead to his own political ruin; as it did.

Jean du Barry hunted around until he discovered somewhere in Navarre a crochety and impoverished old widow, the dowager Comtesse de Bearn. She was a scion of the ancient nobility, the decayed and dying branch of a once mighty tree. She was not only poor to the verge of starvation, but she had a passion for lawsuits. She had just lost a suit, and was on the verge of bankruptcy.

The good-hearted Jean, through the clique's help, arranged to have the case reopened and the decision reversed. This was before our own day of an incorruptible judiciary. He also promised her a gift of twenty thousand dollars in gold. All this in return for the trifling service of journeying up to Paris and thence to Versailles, to act as sponsor for the lovely Madame du Barry, who had wilfully declared that she would be presented under no less auspices than those of the illustrious Comtesse de Bearn.

The old comtesse accepted the offer with all the shrinking reluctance a hungry dog shows at the proffer of a bone.   She came up to Paris, at the expense of the clique, and was immured in Jean's house, with the gambler's sister, Chon (Fanchon) du Barry as her jailer and entertainer.

Choiseul, through his spies, learned of the plot, and he tried in every way to kidnap the old lady or to out-bribe the du Barrys.

Meanwhile, coached by Jean, the fair Marie was making King Louis' life miserable by throwing herself at his feet, in season and out of season, and beseeching him to silence her enemies forever by allowing her to be presented.   When these tactics failed, she would let loose upon the poor king a flood of gutter language, roundly abusing him, turning the air blue with her profanity, and in other ways showing her inalienable right to a place in court circles.

Louis would promise nothing.   The turmoil alter-nately bored and amused him.   At last—April 21, 1769—on his return from the hunt, after an unusually good day's sport, the king casually remarked to all concerned:

"The presentation of Madame la Comtesse du Barry will occur at to-morrow evening's levee."

The traditional and well-thumbed bombshell ex-ploding among them would have created no more stir in court circles than did this yawned announcement. Choiseul and his followers were in despair.   Jean ran around in circles, making preparations for the triumph. Marie rehearsed for the hundredth time the compli-cated forms of etiquette the occasion called for.

The Choiseul faction tried one thing after another to block the ceremony. They kidnapped Marie's hair-dresser, stole the coach in which she was to make the trip from her Paris house to Versailles, arranged a holdup on the road, and so forth. Thanks to Jean's wit and clique's power, a new hairdresser and coach were provided in the nick of time. And the Versailles road was so heavily guarded that a regiment of cavalry could scarce have dared intercept the carriage.

According to one story, Choiseul even got a mes-sage past all the carefully reared barriers to Madame de Bearn, prevailing on her to plead agonized illness and to keep to her bed on the evening set for the presentation. Whereupon, so runs the yarn, a char-acter actor from the Comedie Francaise was paid to "make up" as Madame de Bearn and to perform her functions of sponsor. This may or may not be true. It forms the central theme of De Vere Stacpoole's novel, "The Presentation."

On the great night, the court was assembled, tensely waiting for Marie to arrive. At the appointed time— no Madame du Barry appeared. The minutes grew into an hour; people began to whisper and fidget; the Choiseul party looked blissful; the clique could not hide its worry. Louis stood, frowning, between the suspense stricken D'Aiguillon and Richelieu. At last he turned from them and stared moodily out of a window. Then, moving back into the room, he opened his lips to declare the levee at an end. As he started to speak, an usher announced:

"Madame la Comtesse de Bearn! Madame la Comtesse du Barry!"

And Marie entered, with her sponsor—or with some one who looked sufficiently like Madame de Bearne to deceive any one.

According to one version, Marie was late because at the last instant another Choiseul obstacle had to be cleared away. According to another, she was purposely late to enhance the dramatic interest of her arrival. Here is an account of the presentation:

Madame du Barry, with her chaperon, advanced to where the king stood between their graces, the Ducs of Richelieu and Aiguillon. The formal words were spoken, and Madame du Barry sank to the ground before the king in a profound curtsy. He raised her right hand courteously, his lips twitching with laughter. . . .

She was decked in jewels, priced at nineteen thousand dollars, the gift of the king. She was garbed in one of the triumphant gowns that the women of the hour termed a "fighting dress." So radiant an apparition was she, so dazzling at the first minute of surprise, that even her enemies could not libel her beauty. After she was presented to the king, she was duly presented to Mesdames, to the Dauphin, to the Children of France.

Marie had won. For the next five years she was

the real Queen of France. And, during that time, she cost the French nation, in cold cash. something over seven million dollars.

She was not at all on the style of the Pompadour, who had yearned to meddle in politics. Marie cared nothing for politics, except to help out her army of friends and dependents. She had no ambitions. She had not even craved on her own account to be the king's **maitresse en titre.** All she wanted was to have a good time. And she had it. The pleasure was all hers. The French people did the paying; until, years later, they exacted bloody settlement of the score.

Pompadour had worn out her life trying to "amuse the unamusable," to find novelties that would entertain the king. Marie did nothing of the sort. Instead, she demanded that the king amuse her. Pompadour had sought to sway the destinies of nations. Marie was quite happy if she could spend the revenues of her own nation.

She treated Louis in a way that caused the court to gasp with horror. She scolded him shrilly; petted him, in public, as if he had been her peasant spouse; and always addressed him as "France." He enjoyed it. It was a novelty.

Once, when she was giving an informal breakfast with a dozen or more nobles as guests, she ordered the king to make the coffee. Amused, he obeyed. She took one sip of the royal-brewed beverage, then tossed the cup into the fireplace, exclaiming:

"France, your coffee is as insipid as your talk!"

All political matters she turned over to d'Aiguillon, who was the clique's spokesman.   To please him, and to "get even" for old scores, she caused the ruin of Choiseul.

The mode of Choiseul's downfall is interesting as a side light on court intrigue.   The clique taught Marie how to poison the king's ever-suspicious mind against the prime minister, and she did so with great success. Thanks to her, Louis was held to believe that Choiseul, feeling his power over the monarch slipping, was planning a war scare with Spain, so that he could prove his seeming worth to the kingdom of France by dispelling the cloud.

The clique—having access, through a spy, to all of Choiseul's correspondence—resorted to a fairly ingenious trick.   At Marie's suggestion, Choiseul's secretary was summoned to the palace.   He was in the clique's pay.   Before the king, he was questioned as to what he knew about Choiseul's affairs.

The man, with an air of mystery, answered that he knew nothing of them, but that he would give his majesty one hint—let the king request Choiseul to write a letter to Spain, assuring that nation of France's peaceful intent.   Should Choiseul do so without comment, it would show he was not plotting a war scare, as charged. But should he hesitate—well, what could that prove, instead?

The plotters already knew that Choiseul had that

very day sent a letter to Spain, proposing the mutual signing of a declaration of peace between the nations. The king requested his minister to send a letter that was almost identical with the one he had already written and dispatched. Naturally Choiseul hesitated. And the work was done.

Yet, out of careless good nature—she would not have bothered to harm anybody, politically or otherwise, if she had had her own way—Marie insisted that the king settle a liberal pension on the fallen minister; this despite the fact that Choiseul and his sister, Madame de Grammont, had both worked with all their might and main to block her rise.

She was good, too—as they all were—to her mother. She presented the horrible old woman with two or three estates and a generous income. She did the same for her titular husband, Guillaume, Comte du Barry. Her lightest fancy was enough to make or wreck any Frenchman. Everybody, high or low, was at her mercy. People of the bluest blood vied for chances to win her favor.

The Chevalier de la Morliere dedicated his book on Fatalism to her. The Duc de Tresmes, calling on her, sent in a note: "The monkey of Madame la Comtesse begs an audience." The Dauphin—afterward Louis XVI.—and Marie Antoinette, the Dauphiness, were forced to abase themselves before this vulgarian woman whom they loathed. She reigned supreme.

Extravagant as Pompadour had been, Marie was

tenfold more so. She not only made the king gratify
her every crazy whim, but she spent much time invent-
ing crazy whims for him to gratify. If anything on
sale was costly enough, she wanted it, whether it was
pretty or hideous. All Marie demanded was that the
article should be beyond the reach of any one else.
In consequence, people who wanted to please her
used to shower her with gifts more noteworthy for cost
and for unusualness than for beauty. And one of
these gifts chanced to be a jet-black and quaintly de-
formed ten-year-old slave boy, from Bengal. The
slave's native name was unpronounceable, and the
Prince of Conti—who had bought him from a sea
captain and presented him to Marie—renamed him
Louis Zamore.

Marie was delighted with the boy—as soon as she
heard the price paid for him, and that he was the only
one of his species in France. She dressed him in out-
landish Eastern garb, and she used to tease him into
screeching rages, as a mischievous child might tease a
monkey. The slave child grew to detest his lovely
owner. Remember Louis Zamore, please. He will
come back into the story.

Here is a correct, but incomplete, list of Marie's
personal expenditures during the five years of her
reign as brevet queen of France:

To goldsmiths and jewelers, four hundred and twenty-four
thousand dollars; to merchants of silks, laces, linens, millinery,

one hundred and forty-seven thousand five hundred dollars; for furniture, pictures, vases, et cetera, twenty-three thousand five hundred dollars; to gilders, sculptors, workers in marble, seventy-five thousand dollars.   On her estate at Luciennes— whose chateau was built in three months by the architect Le- doux, whom she thrust into the Academy for doing it—she spent sixty-five thousand dollars.

The heirs of one firm of creditors were, as late as 1836, still claiming the sum of one hundred and thirty thousand dollars from her estate.   She had "state dresses, hooped dresses, dresses **sur la consideration, robes de toilette;**" dresses costing two hundred dollars, four hundred dollars, six hundred dollars, and one thousand dollars; dresses with a base of silver strewn with clusters of feathers; dresses striped with big bars of gold; mosaic dresses shot with gold and adorned with myrtle; and riding habits of white Indian silk that cost twelve hundred dollars.

She had dresses whose elaborate embroidery alone cost twenty-one hundred dollars.   Her dressing gowns had lace on them worth five hundred dollars and eight hundred dollars.   She had cuffs of lace costing one hundred and twenty-five dollars, point-lace caps valued at three hundred dollars, and **point Argentan** costumes at eighteen hundred dollars.   She ordered gold orna- ments and trinkets of all sorts galore.   Roettiers, the goldsmith, received an order from her for a toilet set of solid gold—for which she had a sudden whim.   The government advanced twelve thousand ounces of gold for it.

Boehmer, the Paris jeweler, knowing of her love for ultra-costly things, made up for her a huge diamond necklace, of a heterogeneous mass of many-carat diamonds, arranged with regard to show and wholly without a thought of good taste. The necklace was so big and so expensive that Marie declared at once she must have it. Louis willingly consented to buy it for her; but he died before the purchase was made, and Boehmer was left with the ugly treasure loop on his hands. Long afterward he tried to sell it to Marie Antoinette. And from that transaction rose the mystery of "The Queen's Necklace," which did much to hasten the French Revolution.

In the spring of 1774, as King Louis and Marie were driving toward Versailles, they saw a pretty girl in a wayside field, gathering grass for her cow. Louis greeted the girl with a fatherly smile. The girl looked back at him with perfect indifference.

Piqued at such unwonted contempt for his royal self, the king got out of his carriage, waddled across to where the girl stood, and kissed her. The reason she had seemed indifferent was because she was dazed. The reason she was dazed was that she was in the early stages of smallpox.

Louis caught the infection and died a few days later.

The first act of Louis XVI.—the king's grandson and successor—was to order Marie to a convent. Later he softened the decree by allowing her to live at Luciennes, or anywhere else outside a ten-mile radius from Paris.

Then it was that the fallen favorite met Cosse once more. And their old-time love story recommenced, this time on a less platonic footing. She kept her title of "Comtesse," and had enough money—as she paid few of her debts—to live in luxury; still beautiful, still loved, still moderately young.

The Revolution burst forth. Marie enrolled herself as a stanch loyalist. Hearing that the king and queen were pressed for funds, she wrote to Marie Antoinette:

Luciennes is yours, madame. All that I possess comes to me from the royal family; I am too grateful ever to forget it. The late king, with a sort of presentiment, forced me to accept a thousand precious objects. I have had the honor of making you an inventory of these treasures—I offer them to you with eagerness. You have so many expenses to meet, and benefits without number to bestow. Permit me, I entreat you, to render unto Cæsar that which is Cæsar's.

When the king and queen were beheaded, she secretly wore black for them. Also, she made a trip to England, where she tried to sell some of her jewels to help the royalist cause. All these things were duly repeated to the revolutionary government by Louis Zamore, her Bengalese servant.

One evening she was expecting a visit from Cosse. But midnight came, and he had not appeared.

"Go down the road," she ordered Zamore, who had

just returned from an errand to Paris, "and see if you can catch sight of him."

"I can show him to you—or part of him—without troubling to do that," retorted Zamore, with sudden insolence.

Whipping one hand from behind his back, he tossed on the floor at Marie's feet the head of her lover. Cosse had been guillotined that day. Zamore, in return for certain information to the government, had received the head as a gift.

The information he had given led to Marie's arrest on the following charges:

"Having wasted the treasures of the state, conspiring with the enemies of the Republic, and having, in London, worn mourning for the late King."

Marie was sentenced to death, on December 7, 1793, and was beheaded the same day. Almost alone of all the Frenchwomen thus put to death, she turned coward at the last. The strain of peasant blood came to the fore. And where aristocrats rode smiling to the scaffold, Marie du Barry behaved like a panic-stricken child. She fell on her knees and begged for her life. She told where every article of value she possessed was buried, in her garden. If she thought thus to buy back her life, she did not understand the souls of such men as her captors.

They heard her to the end, jotting down the directions for finding her treasure. Then she was put into the tumbril, and was started on her way to the scaffold.

The journey led past the old millinery shop where she had once worked. As she caught sight of its sign, she screamed out, twice.

The crowd had long ago grown accustomed to the sight of death. Now they seemed to awaken to the fact that they were about to kill a woman, a wondrous beautiful woman, at that. A sigh of pity ran through the throng. The driver in charge of the tumbril, fearing a riot and a rescue, whipped up the horses and drove on with his load. There were others besides Madame du Barry in the death wagon.

The cart reached the scaffold at four-thirty in the afternoon. Marie was the first to mount the steps to the guillotine.

Says De Goncourt, her biographer:

"They heard her on the steps of the scaffold, lost and desperate, mad with anguish and terror, struggling, imploring, begging for mercy, crying, 'Help! Help!' like a woman being assassinated by robbers."

Then fell the ax edge. And Marie's seven-million-dollar debt to the people of France was paid.

CHAPTER TEN

"THE MOST GORGEOUS LADY BLESSINGTON"

S HE was the ugly duckling of a family of seven beautiful children—the children of queer old "Shiver-the-Frills" Power, of Tipperary. Her name was Marguerite. Her father picked out a pretty name for the homely girl and then considered his duty done.

Marguerite was a great trial to everybody; to her good-looking brothers and lovely sisters; to Shiver-the-Frills. who was bitterly chagrined that his record for beauteous offspring should have been marred by so hideous an exception; to the family governess, who wouldn't even take the trouble to teach her to read; to the neighbors, whose joy in beauty she offended. Altogether. Marguerite was taught to consider herself a mistake. It is a lesson that children learn with pitiful readiness. Perhaps the mystic "Unpardonable Sin" consists in teaching them such a damnable doctrine·

Her father's baptismal name was not really Shiver-the-Frills, though nobody ever spoke of him by any other term. He had been christened Edmund, and he was a squireen of the Tipperary village of Knock-brit. He was a local magistrate, and he fulfilled his magisterial office almost as well as a mad dog might have done.

He had an insane temper. He did not confine this to his home—where he beat his children and servants most unmercifully—but aired it on the bench as well. Notably when, in a rage, he lawlessly commandeered a troop of dragoons and galloped over Tipperary and Waterford Counties with them, hunting down and killing peasants who had stirred his anger to maniac heat by some petty uprising.

He was a dandy—fop—macaroni—toff—whatever you choose, too; in a tarnished and down-at-heel way. And from his habit of eternally shaking out his dirty shirt ruffles and lace wristbands, in order to keep them from hanging limply, he was called "Shiver-the-Frills."

Marguerite's home life was one unbroken hell. Starvation, shabby-genteel rags, beatings, and full-flavored curses were her daily portion. A kind-hearted neighbor, Miss Anne Dwyer, took pity on the poor, abused little ugly duckling and taught her to read and write. But for this, she would have grown up too ignorant to pass the very simplest literacy test.

And an odd use the child proceeded to make of her smattering of education. Before she could spell correctly, she began to write stories. These she would read aloud by the peat smolder, on winter evenings, to her awed brothers and sisters, who looked on such an accomplishment as little short of super-natural.

Wonderful stories she wrote, all about princesses who had all the clothes they could wear and who could afford three square meals, with real butter, every single day of their lives; and about princes who never swore at or beat children or flew into crazy rages or even fluttered dirty ruffles.

The girl's gift at story writing gave her a higher place in the family esteem than she had ever enjoyed before. So did another miracle which came to pass when Marguerite was about twelve. She grew pretty. The ugly duckling, in less than a single year, developed from repulsive homeliness into a striking beauty. In fact, by the time she was fourteen, she was far and away the loveliest of all the "exquisite Power sisters."

Then began her career of super-woman. For, with dawning beauty, came an access of the elusive charm that sets Marguerite's type apart from the rest of womankind. And men were swift to recognize her claim to their worship. The swains whom Shiver-the-Frills allowed to visit his tumble-down mansion paid court to her instead of to her sisters. The fame of her reached the near-by garrison town of Clonmel. and brought a host of young redcoat officers swarming to the Knockbrit house.

Of these officers, two soon put themselves far in the van of all other contestants. They were Captain Mur-

ray and Captain Maurice St. Leger Farmer. Murray
was a jolly, happy-go-lucky, penniless chap, lovable
and ardent. The kindest thing one can say about Captain Farmer is that he was more than half insane.

Marguerite met Captain Murray's courtship more
than halfway. But Shiver-the-Frills told the sighing,
but impecunious, swain to keep off, and ordered Marguerite to marry Farmer, who had a snug fortune.
Marguerite very naturally objected. Shiver-the-Frills
flew into a ready-made rage and frightened the poor
youngster almost to death by his threats of what should
befall her if she did not change her mind.

So, cowed into submission, she meekly agreed to
marry Farmer. And marry him she did, in 1805,
when she was but fifteen.

It was an early marrying age, even in that era of
early marriages. Many years had passed since Sheridan's metrical toast "to the maiden of bashful fifteen."
And, as now, a girl of fifteen was deemed too young
for wedlock. But all this did not deter old Shiver-the-
Frills from a laudable firmness in getting rid of the
daughter he hated. So he married her off—to a man
who ought to have been in an insane asylum; in an
asylum for the criminally insane, at that.

If Marguerite's life at Knockbrit had been unhappy,
her new life was positive torture. Farmer's temper was
worse than Shiver-the-Frill's. And he added habitual
drunkenness to his other allurements.

There is no profit in going into full details of Mar-

guerite's horrible sojourn with him.   One of his milder
amusements was to pinch her until the blood spurted
from her white flesh.   He flogged her as he never dared
flog his dogs.   And he used to lock her for days in an
unheated room, in winter, with nothing to eat or drink.

Marguerite stood it as long as she could.   Then she
ran away.   You can imagine how insufferable she had
found Farmer, when I say she went back by choice to
her father's house.

Shiver-the-Frills greeted the unhappy girl with one
of his dear old rages.   His rage was not leveled at the
cur who had so vilely misused her, but against the
young wife who had committed the crime of deserting
her husband.

Not being of the breed that uses bare fingers to test
the efficiency of buzz-saws, I neither express, nor so
much as dare to cherish in secret, any opinion what-
soever on the theme of Woman's Rights.   But it is a
wholly safe and noncontroversial thing to say that the
fate of woman at large, and especially of husband-de-
serters, today, is paradise by comparison with what it
was a century ago.   For leaving a husband who had
not refused to harbor her, Marguerite became in a
measure an outcast.   She could not divorce Farmer;
she could not make him support her, unless she would
return to him.   She was eyed askance by the elect.
Her own family felt that she was smirched.

Shiver-the-Frills cursed her roundly, and is said to
have assumed the heavy-father role by ordering her to

leave his ramshackle old house. Without money, without protector, without reputation, she was cast adrift.

There was no question of alimony, of legal redress, of freedom; the laws were all on Farmer's side. So was public opinion. Strange to say, no public benefactor even took the trouble to horsewhip the husband. He was not even ostracized from his own circle for his treatment to his girl wife.

Remember, this was in the earliest years of the nineteenth century, and in a country where many people still regarded wife-beating as a healthful indoor sport. Less than three decades had elapsed since a man immortalized by Thackeray had made the proud boast that, during the first year of his married life, he had never, when sober, struck his wife in anger. Nor was it so very long after the Lord Chief Justice of England handed down an official decision that a man might legally "punish his wife with a rod no thicker than his lordship's thumb." Whereat, one woman inquired anxiously whether his lordship chanced to suffer from gouty swelling of the hands. Oh, it was a merry time and a merry land—for women—this "Merrie England of the good old days!"

Marguerite vanished from home, from friends, from family. And a blank space follows. In the lives of scores of super-women—of Lola Montez, Marie de Chevreuse, Lady Hamilton, Adah Menken, Peg Woffington, Adrienne Lecouvreur, even of Cleopatra—there was somewhere a hiatus,—a "dark spot" that they would never afterward consent to illumine. And such a line of asterisks sheared its way across Marguerite's page at this point.

She is next heard of as leading a charmingly un-nun-like existence at Cahair, and, two years later, at Dublin. At the Irish metropolis, she enamored the great Sir Thomas Lawrence, whose portrait of her is one of his most famous paintings, and one that is familiar to nearly everybody. The picture was painted in 1809 when Marguerite was just twenty and in the early prime of her beauty.

She had ever a knack of enslaving army men, and her next wooer—in fact, Lawrence's lucky rival—was an Irish captain, one Jenkins. She and Jenkins fell very seriously in love with each other. There was nothing at all platonic in their relations.

Jenkins was eager to marry Marguerite. And when he found he could not do so, because of the trifling obstacle that her husband was alive, he sought a chance to put Captain Maurice St. Leger Farmer out of the road. But he was a square sort of chap, in his way, this lovelorn Jenkins. He balked at the idea of murder, and a duel would have put him in peril of losing Marguerite by dying. So he let Farmer severely alone, and contented himself by waiting impatiently until the drunken husband-emeritus should see fit to die.

And, until that happy hour should come, he declared that Marguerite was at least his wife in the eyes of Heaven. Startlingly novel mode of gluing together the fragments of a fractured commandment! But the strange part of the affair is that Captain Jenkins' eminently respectable family consented to take the same view of the case and publicly welcomed Marguerite as the captain's legal wife.

And so, for a time, life went on. Marguerite was as nearly respectable as the laws of her time gave her the right to be. Jenkins was all devotion. She was moderately well received in local society, and she kept on winning the hearts of all the men who ventured within her sway.

Then into her life swirled Charles John Gardiner, Earl of Blessington, one of the most eccentric and thoroughly delightful figures of his day.

Blessington was an Irish peer, a widower, a man of fashion. He had a once-enormous rent roll, that had been sadly honeycombed by his mad extravagances, but that still totaled one hundred and fifty thousand dollars a year.

What chance had the worthy, but humble, Captain Jenkins against this golden-tinged whirlwind wooer? And the answer to that conundrum is the same that serves for the question concerning the hackneyed snowball in the Inferno. Blessington swept Marguerite off her feet, bore her away from the protesting captain and installed her in a mansion of her own.

Then, too late, came the happy event for which Jenkins and Marguerite had so optimistically been looking. In October, 1817, Captain Maurice St. Leger

Farmer joined some boon companions in an all-night orgy in the upper room of a pothouse. Farmer waxed so much drunker than usual that he mistook the long window of the room for the door. Bidding his friends good-by, he strolled out of the window into space. Being a heavier-than-air body, in spite of the spirits that buoyed him up, he drifted downward into the courtyard below, breaking his miserable neck.

Marguerite was free. Jenkins hastened to her and besought her to marry him, offering her an honorable name and a place in the world, and pointing out to her how much better off she would be in the long run as Mrs. Captain Jenkins than as the brevet bride of a dissolute earl.

But Blessington had by this time become the helpless thrall of Marguerite's charm. As soon as he heard of Farmer's death, he whisked her off to church and married her. And, by way of doing all things handsomely, he soothed the disconsolate Jenkins' feelings with a fifty-thousand-dollar check; thereby securing firm title to the good will and fixtures of the previous tenant of his wife's heart·

The earl took his new wife to his ancestral home, at Mountjoy Forest. And there the couple kept open house, spending money like drunken sailors, and having a wonderful time. It was the first chance Marguerite had ever had for spending any large amount of money. She so well improved her opportunities along this line, and got such splendid results therefrom, that she was nicknamed by a flowery Irish admirer "the most gorgeous Lady Blessington." And the name stuck to her, to her delight, all through life.

Blessington had always been extravagant. Now, goaded on by Marguerite, he proceeded to make the Prodigal Son look like Gaspard the Miser. One of his lesser expenditures was the building of a theater on his own estate, that he and Marguerite might satisfy to the full their love for amateur theatricals.

At this theater they and their friends were the only performers, and their friends were the only spectators. The performances must have been gems of histrionic and literary excellence, and a rare delight to every one concerned. It would have been worth walking barefoot for miles to witness one of them.

For the actors were bound by a list of hard-and-fast rules devised and written out by Lord Blessington himself. You may judge the rest of these rules by the first, which read:

> Every gentleman shall be at liberty to avail himself of the words of the author, in case his own invention fails him.

One's heart warms to the genius who could frame that glorious rule for stage dialogue.

But Marguerite was of no mind to be mured up in an Irish country house, with perhaps an occasional trip to Dublin. She had begun to taste life, and she found the draft too sweet to be swallowed in sips. She made

Blessington take a house in St. James' Square, in London·

There, for the next three years, she was the reigning beauty of the capital. Her salons were the most brilliant spots in the London season. Her loveliness made her and her home a center of admiration.

She had more than good looks; more, even, than charm. She had brains, and she had true Irish wit; a wit that flashed and never stung. She had, too, the knack of bringing out the best and brightest elements in everyone around her. So, while men adored her, women could not bring themselves to hate her.

She was in her element, there in London. But Blessington was not in his. He enjoyed it all; but he was no longer young, and he had led a lightning-rapid life. So, though he was ever a willing performer, the merciless pace began to tell on him.

Marguerite was quick to notice this. And she suggested that a nice, long, lazy tour of the Continent might brace him up. Marguerite's lightest suggestions were her husband's laws. So to the Continent they went. and London mourned them.

They set off in August, 1822. "No Irish nobleman," says one biographer, "and certainly no Irish king, ever set out on his travels with such a retinue of servants, with so many vehicles and appliances of all kinds to ease, to comfort, and the luxurious enjoyment of travel."

They planned to go by easy stages, stopping wher-

ever they chose and for as long as the fancy held them.
They traveled in a way a modern pork-king might
envy.

One day in Paris, at the races, Lady Blessington
exclaimed:

"There is the handsomest man I have ever
seen!"

One of the throng of adorers hanging about the
Blessington box confessed to knowing the stranger,
and he was accordingly sent off posthaste to bring the
"handsomest man" to the box. The personage who
was so lucky as to draw forth this cry of admiration
from Marguerite was at that time but eighteen years
old. Yet already he was one of the most noted—or
notorious—men-about-town in all Europe.

He was Alfred Guillaume Gabriel, Count d'Orsay,
a typical Ouida hero. He was six feet in height, with
broad shoulders, small hands and feet, hazel eyes, and
chestnut hair. He was an all-round athlete—could
ride, fence, box, skate, shoot,—and so on, through the
whole list of sports. He was a brilliant conversation-
alist. He could draw. He could paint. He was a
sculptor. And at none of these things was he an amateur, but as good as most front-rank professionals. He
was later to win fame as the premier man of fashion
of the period. A once celebrated book, "The Complete
Dandy," had d'Orsay for its hero. Everybody who
came in touch with the youthful paragon fell victim
to his magnetism, and even Lord Blessington—who

should have been wise enough to see what was coming —was no exception.

Young D'Orsay, at Marguerite's instigation, was invited to go along with the Blessingtons on the rest of their travels. He accepted. This meant his resignation from his regiment, which was at that moment under orders to leave France to invade Spain. He threw over his military career without a qualm. He had fallen in love at sight with "the most gorgeous Lady Blessington," who was fourteen years his senior. And, at sight, she had fallen in love with him. It was the love of her life·

The party moved on to Genoa. Here they met Lord Byron, who had found England a chilly abiding place, after the disgraceful affair that had parted him from his wife. Byron was charmed by Lady Blessington's beauty and cleverness, and spent a great deal of time with the Blessington party of tourists.

D'Orsay he liked immensely, once referring to him as "a Greek god returned to earth." Marguerite he frankly adored. And—so far as one knows—that was all the good it did him. With a wonder youth of the D'Orsay type ever at her side, Lady Blessington was not likely to lose her sophisticated heart to a middle-aged, lame man, whose power over women was at this time largely confined to girls in their teens. But Byron was the greatest living poet, as well as the greatest living charlatan. And Marguerite consented to be amused, in desultory fashion, by his stereotyped form of heart siege; even though his powers of attack were no longer sufficient to storm the citadel.

Still, the time passed pleasantly enough at Genoa; and Byron salved his bruised vanity by wheedling Lord Blessington into buying his yacht—a boat that the poet had long and vainly tried to get rid of. Faring better with "my lord" than with "my lady," he sold the boat at a fancy figure.

There was a farewell banquet, at which he drank much. Then the Blessingtons and D'Orsay departed from Genoa—on the white-elephant yacht. And Byron stood on the quay and wept aloud as they sailed off.

They went to Rome. But the Eternal City somehow did not appeal to Lady Blessington. So they gave it what would now be vulgarly termed "the once over," and passed on to Naples. Here, Marguerite was delighted with everything. The trio took a Naples house, and lived there for two and a half years·

The mansion Lord Blessington rented was the Palazzo Belvidere—which cost him an enormous sum. But, like an automobile, the initial price was the smallest item of its expense. Marguerite, perhaps to atone to herself for the squalor of her rickety girlhood home, declared the place would not be fit to live in until it had been refitted according to her ideas. Her ideas cost a fortune to carry out. But when at last the work was done, she wrote that the palazzo was "one of the most delicious retreats in the world." She also hit on

a thoroughly unique, if costly, scheme for sight-seeing.
For example, when she visited Herculaneum, it was
with the archæologist, Sir William Gell, as guide.
When she went to museums and art galleries, she took
along as showman such celebrities as Unwin, the painter, Westmacott, the sculptor, or the antiquary, Milli-
gan.   And when she visited the observatory, it was
under the guidance of Sir John Herschel and the
Italian astronomer Piazzi.   More than one of these
notables sighed hopelessly for her love.

From Naples the party went to Florence·   Here
Walter Savage Landor met Marguerite.   And he was
little behind Byron in his appreciation of her charms.

By this time—nay, long before this time—people
had begun to talk, and to talk quite distinctly.   Marguerite did not care to be the butt of international gossip, so she enlisted her husband's aid in an effort to
silence the scandalous tongues.   Blessington's mode of
doing this was highly characteristic of the most eccentric man living.   He promptly offered to make D'Orsay his heir, if the latter would marry Lord Blessington's fifteen-year-old-daughter, the earl's only living
child by his first wife.   D'Orsay did not object.   It
mattered little to him whom he married.   The girl was
sent for to come to Florence, and there she and D'Orsay were made man and wife.

The trio thus enlarged to a quartet, all hands next
set off for Paris.   Lady Blessington learned that the
house of Marechal Ney was vacant, and she made

her husband take it at a staggering rental.   And again she was not satisfied until the place had been done over from top to bottom.   The job was finished in three days, the army of workmen receiving triple pay for quadruple speed.   Lady Blessington's own room was designed by her husband.   He would not allow her to see it until everything was in readiness for her.   This is her own description of it:

The bed, which is silvered instead of gilt, rests on the backs of two large silver swans, so exquisitely sculptured that every feather is in alto-relievo, and looks nearly as fleecy as those of a living bird.   The recess in which it is placed is lined with white fluted silk, bordered with blue embossed lace; and from the columns that support the frieze of the recess, pale-blue silk curtains, lined with white, are hung; which, when drawn, conceal the recess altogether.   .   .   .   A silvered sofa has been made to fit the side of the room opposite the fireplace.

Pale-blue carpets, silver lamps, ornaments silvered to correspond.   .   .   .   The salle de bain is draped with white muslin trimmed with lace.   .   .   .   The bath is of white marble, inserted in the floor, with which its surface is level.   On the ceiling a painting of Flora scattering flowers with one hand, while from the other is suspended an alabaster lamp in the form of a lotus.

It was in this house that Lord Blessington died, of apoplexy, in 1829; perhaps after a glimpse of the bills for renovating the place.

Marguerite, on his death, was left with a jointure in his estate—which estate by this time had dwindled to fifty thousand dollars per annum. Her sole share of it was seven-thousand-five-hundred dollars a year, and the Blessington town house in London.

All along, D'Orsay and his wife had been living with the Blessingtons. When Lady Blessington came back to England, they accompanied her, and the three took up their odd form of life together at Gore House, in Kensington—Albert Hall now stands on its site— for Marguerite could not afford to keep up the Blessington mansion.

She tried to eke out her income by writing, for she still had the pen gift that had so awed her brothers and sisters. One of her first pieces of work was a book based on her talks with Byron, back in the Genoa days. The **New Monthly Magazine** first printed serially this capitalization of a dead romance. The volume later came out as "Conversations With Byron." And, of all Marguerite's eighteen books, this is, perhaps, the only one now remembered.

She was engaged, at two-thousand-five-hundred dollars a year, to supply a newspaper with society items. Then, too, she edited "Gems of Beauty," a publication containing portraits of fair women, with a descriptive verse written by her under each picture—straight hack work. Altogether, she made about five thousand dollars a year by her pen; a goodly income for a woman writer in her day—or in any day, for that matter.

Among her novels were "Meredith," "Grace Cas-

sidy," "The Governess," and "The Victims of Society."
You have never read any of them, I think. If you tried
to, as did I, they would bore you as they bored me.
They have no literary quality; and their only value is
in their truthful depiction of the social life of her
times.

She did magazine work, too, and wrote for such
chaste publications as **Friendship's Offering, The Amu-
let, Keepsakes,** and others of like mushiness of name
and matter.

Once more her salons were the talk of all England,
and once more the best men crowded to them. But no
longer did the best women frequent the Blessington
receptions. The scandal that had been hushed by
the sacrifice of the earl's daughter to a man who loved
her stepmother had blazed up fresh when the D'Orsays
went to live at Gore House with Marguerite. And
women fought shy of the lovely widow.

It is one of the mysteries of the ages that so canny an
old libertine as Lord Blessington should have been
hood-winked by D'Orsay and Marguerite. There is
no clew to it, except—perhaps he was not fooled. Perhaps he was too old, too sick, too indifferent to care.

And when D'Orsay's unhappy young wife, in 1838,
refused to be a party any longer to the disgusting farce
and divorced her husband, the gossip-whispers swelled
to a screech. The wife departed; D'Orsay stayed
on.

There is every reason to think Marguerite was true

to her young "Greek God." But if so, it was not for lack of temptation or opportunity to be otherwise. In her late forties and early fifties, she was still "the most gorgeous Lady Blessington," still as lovely, as magnetic, as adorable as in her teens.

Among the men who delighted to honor her salons with their frequent presence—and more than one of them made desperate love to their hostess—were Bulwer, Dickens, Thackeray, Sir Robert Peel, Captain Marryat, Brougham, Landseer, Tom Moore, Disraeli, and many another genius.

Disraeli—one day to rule British politics as Lord Beaconsfield—was at that time merely a brilliant politician and an almost equally brilliant novelist. There is a story—I don't vouch for it—that, piqued at Marguerite's coldness toward himself, Disraeli revenged himself by portraying D'Orsay right mercilessly as "Count Mirabeau," in his "Henrietta Temple."

Landor was drawn by her lure into returning to England. The aged Duke of Wellington, too, was a guest at her more informal "at homes." Marguerite used such influence as she possessed over the duke to persuade him to let D'Orsay paint his portrait. So well did the picture turn out that the duke cried in delight:

"At last I've been painted as a gentleman!"

To the Blessington salons came an American, a man whose clothes were the hopeless envy of Broadway, and whose forehead curl was imitated by every Yankee dandy who could afford to buy enough pomatum to stick a similar curl to his own brow. He was N. P. Willis. You don't even start at the name. Yet that name used to thrill your grandmother. Willis was a writer; and gained more temporary fame for less good work than any other author our country has produced.

During a tour of England, he was fortunate enough to receive an invitation to call on Lady Blessington. And thereafter he called almost every day. He fairly raved over her.

"She is one of the most lovely and fascinating women I have ever known!" he wrote.

Then he wrote more; he wrote a story of something that happened at one of her soirees. He sent it to an American paper, never dreaming it would ever be seen in England. But the story was reprinted in an English magazine. And D'Orsay showed Willis the door.

Another visitor to Gore House was a pallid, puffy princeling, out of a job and out of a home. He was Louis Napoleon, reputed nephew of Napoleon the Great; and he was one day to reign as Napoleon III., Emperor of the French. In the meantime, exiled from France, he knocked around the world, morbidly wondering where his next suit of ready-made clothes was to come from. He even visited the United States, for a while, teaching school at Bordentown, New Jersey, and sponging for loans and dinners from the Jumels and other people kindly disposed to the Bonaparte cause.

Just now he was in England, living, when he could, on borrowed money, and sometimes earning a few shillings by serving as special policeman outside of big houses where dances or receptions were in progress. Out of the few English homes open to the prince was Marguerite Blessington's.

Marguerite and D'Orsay took him in, fed him, lent him money, and did a thousand kindnesses to the poor, outlawed fellow. You shall learn in a few minutes how he repaid their generosity.

While Marguerite had a talent for writing, she had a positive genius for spending money. And where talent and genius clash, there can be only one final result. Her talent, as I have said, brought her about five thousand dollars a year. Her income from her husband's estate was a yearly seven-thousand-five-hundred dollars more. But how could people like Marguerite and D'Orsay keep abreast of the social current on a beggarly twelve-thousand-five-hundred dollars a year?

The foregoing is a question, not a flight of rhetoric. It has an answer. And the answer is: they went into debt.

They threw away money; as apt pupils of the lamented Earl of Blessington might readily have been expected to. When they had no more money to pay with, they got credit. At first, this was easy enough.

Tradesmen, high and low, deemed it an honor to be creditors of the all-popular Dowager Countess of Blessington, and of the illustrious Count D'Orsay.   And even after the tradesmen's first zest died down, the couple were clever enough to arrange matters in such a way as to keep right on securing goods for which they knew they never could hope to pay.

Stripped of his glamour, his pretty tricks, and his social position, D'Orsay shows up as an unadulterated dead beat, a sublimated panhandler; while Marguerite's early experience in helping Shiver-the-Frills ward off bailiffs and suchlike gold-seekers now stood her in fine stead.

They were a grand pair.   Their team-work was perfect.   Between them, they succeeded in rolling up debts amounting to more than five-hundred-and-thirty-five-thousand dollars to tradesfolk alone.   D'Orsay, in addition to this, managed to borrow about sixty-five thousand from overtrustful personal friends.

Thackeray is said to have drawn from them the inspiration of his "Vanity Fair" essay on "How to Live on Nothing a Year."   D'Orsay, before consenting to let his wife divorce him, had stipulated that the earl's daughter pay him a huge lump sum out of the Blessington estate.   He was also lucky at so-called games of chance, and his painting brought in a good revenue. But all this money was swallowed up in the bottomless gulf of extravagance.

Little by little, the tradesmen began to realize that

they were never going to be paid, and they banded together to force matters to a crisis. In that era, debt was still punishable by imprisonment. and prison gates were almost ready to unbar in hospitable welcome to Marguerite and D'Orsay.

Like Dick Swiveller, who shut for himself, one by one, every avenue of egress, from his home, by means of unpaid-for purchases in neighboring streets, D'Orsay discovered that it was no longer safe to leave the house. Officers with warrants lurked at the area railings of Gore House. Tipstaves loitered on the front steps. All sorts of shabby people seemed eager to come into personal contact with Alfred Guillaume Gabriel, Count D'Orsay.

On Sunday alone—when the civil arm of the law rests—did the much-sought-after couple dare emerge from the once-joyous house which had grown to be their beleaguered castle. No longer could they entertain, as of yore, lest a rascally warrant-server slip into the drawing-room in the guise of a guest.

Finally, the net tightened to such an extent that D'Orsay had great ado to slip through its one gap; but slip through he did, and escaped by night to France. Marguerite's wit arranged for his escape. And the man who lately had disdained to take a week-end journey without a half-dozen servants and a half score trunks was forced to run away in the clothes he wore. and with single portmanteau. Marguerite joined him at Boulogne, little better equipped than he.

Oh, but there were heartbreaking sights, in those days, in Boulogne, in Calais, and in Havre! Englishmen who had fled their own country for debt used to haunt the French seaboard, as being nearer their own dear land than was Paris. They used to pace the esplanades or cower like sick dogs on the quays, straining their eyes across the tumbled gray water, to glimpse the far-off white cliffs of their homeland. They would flock to the pier, when the Channel packets came in, longing for the sight of a home face, dreading to be seen by some one who had known them in sunnier days. Sneered at by the thrifty French, denied a penny's worth of credit at the shops, they dragged out desolate lives, fifty times more bitter than death.

It was no part of Marguerite's scheme to enroll D'Orsay and herself among these hangdog exiles. She had ever built air-castles, and she was still building them. She had wonderful plans for a career in France.

She and D'Orsay had done much for Louis Napoleon in his days of poverty. And now Louis Napoleon was President of France, and already there were rumors that he would soon make himself emperor. He was the Man of the Hour. And in his heyday of prosperity he assuredly could do no less than find a high government office for D'Orsay and pour a flood of golden coin into the lap of "the most gorgeous Lady Blessington."

Let me save you from suspense by telling you that

Louis Napoleon did nothing of the sort. Indeed, he seemed much embarrassed and not at all over-joyed by the arrival of his old benefactors in Paris. He made them many glittering promises. But the Bank of Fools itself would have had too much sense to discount such promises as Louis Napoleon was wont to make.

Soon after their arrival in Paris, Marguerite learned that creditors had swooped down upon Gore House, seizing it and all the countless art treasures that filled it. House and contents went under the hammer, and brought a bare sixty thousand dollars; not enough to pay one of the D'Orsay-Blessington debts.

Marguerite was at the end of her career. She was sixty years old; her beauty was going; her money was gone. She had ruled hearts; she had squandered fortunes; she had gone through the "dark spot," (ninety-nine per cent of whose victims sink thence to the street, while the hundredth has the amazing luck to emerge as a Super-Woman.) She had listened to the love vows of men whose names are immortal. And now she was old and fat and banished. Hope was dead.

A younger and stronger woman might readily have succumbed under such a crisis. Certainly, Marguerite Blessington was in no condition to face it. Soon after she arrived in Paris, she sickened and died.

D'Orsay had loved her with fairly good constancy, and he designed in her honor a double-grave mausoleum of quaint design. And under that mausoleum, at Chambourey, she was buried. Three years later, D'Orsay was laid there at her side.

Super-woman and super-man, they had loved as had Cleopatra and Antony. Only, in the latters' day, it was Rome's vengeance and not a creditor-warrant that cut short such golden romances.

CHAPTER XI

MADAME RECAMIER

THE FROZEN-HEARTED ANGEL

PARIS—the hopelessly mixed, **sans-culotte**-philoso-
pher new Paris society of 1793—took a holiday
from red slaughter and reflection on the Rights
of Man, and went to an odd wedding.

The wedding of a fifteen-year-old girl to a man of
nearly fifty. Probably. even in that less bromidic day,
there were not lacking a few hundred guests to com-
mit the ancient wheeze anent May and December. The
girl was a beauty of the type that it tightens one's
throat to look at. And the man was an egregiously
rich banker. So Paris deigned to be interested;
interested even into momentary forgetfulness of the
day's "List of the Condemned" and of Robespierre's
newest patriotic murder dreams.

The girl bride was Jeanne Francoise Julie Adelaide
Bernard, daughter of no less a dignitary than the Paris'
receiver of taxes—a mild-mannered and handsome
man, weak and stupid, with a handsome and steel-
eyed wife, who was neither dull, weak, nor good.

The groom was Jacques Recamier—by profession a powerful banker, by choice a middle-class Lothario. His father had sold hats at Lyons. Recamier had been an intimate friend of the Bernards, forever at their house, since a year or so before Jeanne had been born.

As the wedding party stood on the steps of the Hotel de Ville, after the "civil ceremony"—so runs the story—a passing man halted and gazed long and closely at Jeanne, in dumb admiration, studying every line of her face and form. The gazer was a painter, Greuze by name. And from Jeanne Recamier, as he saw her that day, he drew the inspiration for the wonderful **"Jeune fille"** picture that made him immortal.

The wedding party filed into a line of waiting carriages. But scarce had the joyous cavalcade set out on its short journey when it was halted by the passage of a truly horrible procession that just then emerged from a cross street; a procession made up of scarecrow men and women, hideous of visage, clad in rags, blood from the guillotine—around which they had lately gathered, gloating—spattered on their clothes and unwashed faces.

In the midst of the howling and huzzaing throng was a chair, carried by supports on the shoulders of eight half-naked **sans-culottes.** And in this lofty chair crouched the most hideous figure in all that vile gathering—a dwarfish, weirdly dressed man, his face disgustingly marred by disease, his eyes glaring with the light of madness.

Around him gamboled the mob, screaming blessings and adulations, strewing his bearers' way with masses of wilted flowers, filched from the **halles.**

Thus did Doctor Jean Paul Marat make his triumphal return home that April day from the Convention, escorted by his worshipers—and fellow beasts. Thus did his obscene retinue block the wedding procession of dainty little Jeanne Recamier. Jean Paul Marat— for whose shrunken chest, at that very moment, poor, politics-crazed Charlotte Corday was sharpening the twenty-eight-cent case knife she had just bought.

An odd omen for the outset of married life; and vitally so to the little new-wed Recamier girl, who had been brought up amid superstitions.

Shall we glance at a short word picture of Jeanne, limned by a contemporary?

"She has orange-tinted eyes, but they are without fire; pretty and transparent teeth, but incapable of snapping; an ungainly waist; coarse hands and feet; and complexion that is a bowl of milk wherein float rose leaves."

Let me add to the sketch the established fact that, during the seventy-one years of her life, no man so such as boasted that he had received a caress or a love word from her. But don't lose interest in her, please, on that account. Dozens of men would blithely have tossed away their souls for the privilege of making that boast truthfully. Failing, they nicknamed her "the angel of the frozen heart." Against her, alone, perhaps of all super-women, no word of scandal was ever breathed. (Chiefly, it has been claimed, for physical reasons.)

Let me touch, as brieflly as I can, on a story at which Madame Lenormand, her own cousin, broadly hints and which Turquan openly declares true. Says the former, among other and closer comments on the theme:

"Madame Recamier received from her husband but his name. His affection was paternal. He treated as a daughter the woman who carried his name."

Says Turquan:

"She was Recamier's daughter."

And so, by all testimony, she was. Years before, Recamier had had a love affair with Madame Bernard; an affair that the stupid Bernard had condoned, if he had known of its existence. Nor, said gossip of the day, was it Madame Bernard's sole indiscretion.

Jeanne had been born. From her earliest babyhood, Recamier had all but worshiped her. Not a day had passed but he had come to see her. He had loaded her with toys, jewelry, candy. He had been her fairy godfather. She had grown up calling him "Daddy Recamier."

Then came the Reign of Terror. Old Bernard's life was in considerable danger. In fact he used to go to the guillotine daily to watch executions, "that he might become used to his fate." Madame Bernard was no fit guardian for a young and incredibly lovely girl in the rotten Paris of that day.

So Recamier, rich and powerful, chose the surest means to safeguard the daughter who was all the world to him. He went through a meaningless "civil ceremony" with her; and installed her, with a retinue of servants, in one-half of his big house. Then and thereafter she was Madame Recamier in name alone; Recamier tenderly watching over her, giving her every luxury money could buy, and observing with a total absence of jealousy her innumerable conquests.

These conquests had begun, by the way, even before Jeanne's early marriage. When she was but thirteen, a young man named Humblot had fallen madly in love with her. To keep Jeanne from reciprocating his flame, she had been packed off to a convent school.

Shortly after the marriage, the Reign of Terror simmered down to the more peaceful if more corrupt Directory. Society reassembled on its peak, after the years of guillotine-aided class leveling. And, in this heterogeneous society, Jeanne blazed forth as a star. Says Sainte-Beuve:

"The world Madame Recamier traversed at this period was very mixed and very ardent."

To its adoration the girl bride lent an amused but wholly impersonal ear. Vaguely she used to wonder why men wept at her feet and poured forth their souls in noisy love for her. Their antics found no response in her own untouched heart. Yet she found them interesting, and therefore in a demure way she encouraged them. Not that such encouragement was really needed.

Presently, out of the chaos of social and political conditions, arose Napoleon Bonaparte. Yes, I know he appears unduly often in this series. But he appeared unduly often in the lives of a score of superwomen—Madame Jumel, Elizabeth Paterson, Madamoiselle Georges, Countess Potocka, and the rest—and his name is more often seen in all history, written since 1790, than that of any other man. So be patient if he crops up oftener than the balance of power seems to call for.

Napoleon, first as dictator and then as emperor, ruled France. As a young man, he had been too poor and too busy to glance at any woman. Now in his days of power and—for him—leisure, he amply made up for such early defects. And presently his alternately pale and jet-black eyes fell upon Jeanne Recamier. Forthwith, he began to make right ardent love to her.

Napoleon, once and only once in all his strange career, had actually lost his level head through love and had been carried by it out of his cool, calculating self. That was when, as a lean, half-starved, hectic young officer of artillery, he had met Josephine Beauharnais.

She was a Creole widow, much older than he. Much slush has been written of her and her wrongs. History, from every source, tells another story.

Napoleon used to meet Josephine at the house of the director, Barras, where she held a somewhat equivocal position. Barras had begun to tire of her. Her teeth were bad; she was beginning to wrinkle and grow sallow; she was silly; she had absolutely nothing in common with the late Mrs. Cæsar.

To Napoleon, though, she was as a third-rate show to a country boy who had never before visited the theater. She was divine. Barras saw; and he also saw a chance to rid himself of a burden and at the same time to attach to himself a growingly useful friend.

Barras persuaded Josephine to marry Napoleon—whom she did not even pretend to love—by saying that the young man had a great future. Then, as a wedding present, he gave Napoleon command of the ragged, mutinous Army of Italy.

Napoleon, after turning that army into such a fighting machine as the world had never before known, thrashed Italy and Austria and came home the hero and idol of the hour—to find, beyond all doubt or hope, that Josephine was unfaithful to him! He ordered her out of his house. She wept. Her family wept. Every one wept. Every one pleaded. Napoleon shrugged his shoulders and let her stay. But ever thereafter he treated her with mere friendly tolerance. His love for her was stone-dead. And he amused himself wherever amusement could be found.

Also, when it suited his turn in after years, he calmly divorced her.

"Lefebvre," said Napoleon, in Egypt, "what is Josephine doing at this moment?"

"Weeping for your return," promptly babbled the future Duke of Dantzig.

"Lefebvre," soulfully returned Napoleon, "you're a fool or a liar! Or both. She is riding a white horse in the Bois, in the worst kind of company she can find at such short notice."

Men of rank and wit were choking Madame Recamier's salon to overflowing. She was the inaccessible goal of a hundred Don Juans' ambitions. Grandees of the old and the new regime as well—aristocrats of the noblesse—who would not deign to visit the Tuileries while the Corsican adventurer held sway in that house of kings—all flocked to the Recamier home and vied with one another to do Jeanne honor.

Her beauty, her siren charm, her snowy—or frosty —virtue were the talk of France. What more natural than that Napoleon should seek out this new paragon; that sheer conceit as well as genuine love should make him burn to succeed where all the world had failed?

Other women—women whose houses he could not have entered, seven years earlier, save as a dependent —were making fools of themselves over the Man of Destiny. He had but to throw the handkerchief for a hundred frail beauties to scramble for its possession. Irresistible, perfect in power and in the serene know-

ledge of that power, he deigned to make lazy love to
Jeanne Recamier.

She was not used to lazy love-making. She did not
understand it, but took it for a mere new mannerism
of the hypermanneristic emperor. Her seeming indifference had the same effect on Napoleon as might
a war campaign that promised grave obstacles. It
turned his idle fancy to keen pursuit. Madame Recamier failed to be impressed. Napoleon, thinking
he must be mistaken in the idea that any living woman
could fail to be dazzled by his attentions, made his
meaning quite clear. Only to meet with a very good-
humored but extremely definite rebuff from his
charmer.

It was past his understanding. He stooped to
bribes; offering to put a big share of the state finances
through the Recamier bank, and, with much pomp and
ceremony, announcing the appointment of Madame
Recamier as one of the Empress Josephine's ladies in
waiting.

This was a master stroke—a **tour de force**—a
knock-out—anything you will. For, fat and curved-
nosed bankers throughout the empire were yelping for
slices of the state finances. And the post of lady in
waiting was one for which nearly any woman of the
court would gladly have parted with all she no longer
possessed.

Then came a shock; a rough, jarring shock; a
shock worthy to be administered by, instead of to, the

Corsican himself. Madame Recamier coldly refused
the glittering offers; declined to be a lady in waiting;
and gave Napoleon to understand, in terms he could
not mistake, that she wanted nothing from him except
unadulterated absence.

It was probably the emperor's one heart rebuff.

In a burst of babyish fury, he——the ruler of France
and the arbiter of Europe's fate——crawled so low as
to seek revenge on a harmless woman.

He first wrecked the Recamier bank, driving old
Recamier to the verge of ruin. Then he trumped
up an asinine charge of treason or **lese majeste** or
something equally absurd, against Jeanne. And on the
strength of it, he banished her from Paris.

It was a revenge well worthy the eccentric who
could rule or ruin half of Europe by a single convolu-
tion of his demigod brain; or could screech in impotent
fury at a valet for getting the wrong part in his thin hair.

From Paris went the Recamiers; the banker seeking gently to console his unhappy wife for the ruin she
had so innocently wrought; and to build up for her,
bit by bit, a new fortune to replace the lost one. Never
by word or look did he blame her. And speedily he
amassed enough money to supply her again with the
luxuries she loved.

To Lyons, the old home of both of them, they went;
thence to Rome, and then to Naples. In Italy, Jeanne
met once more her dearest woman friend; a ludicrously
homely woman with the temper of a wet cat and a

tongue sharp enough to shave with; a complete foil, mentally and facially, for her bosom friend, Jeanne.

This miracle of homeliness was Madame de Stael, author and futile conspirator. For exercising the latter accomplishment, she had been banished, like Jeanne, from Paris. So ugly was Madame de Stael that when she once said to an ill-favored man:

"You abuse the masculine prerogative of homeliness," her hearers laughed—at her, not at her victim.

In Italy, too, Jeanne met Prince Augustus of Prussia, prince-royal and man of distinction and wealth. They met at a reception. Madame Recamier and Madame de Stael were seated side by side on a sofa. After the introductions, Prince Augustus seated himself between them, remarking airily:

"I find myself placed between Wit and Beauty."

"And possessing neither," commented Madame de Stael, with her wonted courtesy.

The prince, from that inauspicious start, became the infatuated slave of Madame Recamier. He worshiped the ground she trod. He made no secret of his devotion.

In those days the title of prince-royal carried real weight, and the gulf between prince and commoner was well-nigh unbridgeable. Love made Prince Augustus waive all this disparity. The fact that Madame Recamier was a mere commoner grew to mean nothing to him. At the risk of disgrace at home and of possible loss of rank and fortune, the prince entreated Jeanne to divorce Recamier and to marry his royal-blooded self.

It was a brilliant offer, one that ninety-nine commoners out of a hundred would have seized with alacrity; for it was not a morgantic union he proposed —he wanted to make Jeanne his princess.

The prince went to Recamier and frankly stated his wishes. To his amaze, instead of challenging the wooer, Recamier at once agreed to let Jeanne get the divorce, on any grounds she chose—or an annulment of their marriage, which would have been still simpler —and marry Prince Augustus.

Always impersonal and adoring in his attitude toward Jeanne, Recamier now urged her to secure her own best interests by giving him up and becoming the prince's wife; a sacrifice far easier to understand in a father than in a husband.

But Jeanne put aside the offer without a tremor of hesitation, turning her back on the wealth and title of a princess in order to remain with the bankrupt old commoner whom the world called her husband. For, again, physical reasons intervened.

Lucien Bonaparte, one of the emperor's several brothers, was another ardent wooer. He shone in reflected glory. as his brother's brother, until he seemed quite royal. But to him. as to all the rest, Jeanne— after a wholly harmless and pleasant flirtation—gave a decided refusal.

General Bernadotte, on a foreign mission for the

emperor, sought her out. He was a military chief who had fought like a hero and on whom court honors had since fallen thick. He sought. soldier fashion, to carry Jeanne's icy defenses by storm; only to fail as all had failed and to go home grumbling that his majesty had done well to exile so unapproachable a beauty before she had a chance to drive every man in France mad with chagrin.

Benjamin Constant, too—cunning statesman of the old school—loved her. And in his strange, unfathomable mind she found a certain fascination; the more so when she discovered that she could twist that mind to her own purposes. So, instead of dismissing Constant like the rest, she made it clear that she did not love him and then kept him as a friend.

Strong use did she make of that friendship, too, in revenging herself on Napoleon for banishing her. Constant's mighty if tortuous acts of statescraft, just before and just after Napoleon's downfall, have been laid to her influence.

Another exile—General Moreau, Napoleon's ofttime rival in both war and love—now sought to win where his enemy had lost. And he failed. He was the same General Moreau who a few years earlier had paid court to Betty Jumel and had given her as a love gift a huge gilt-and-prism chandelier which later hung in the Jumel mansion in New York. But he found Jeanne as cold as Betty had been kind, and in time he, too, departed, hopeless.

The next victim was no less a personage than the
King of Naples.   He was Murat, ex-tavern waiter,
peerless cavalry leader, and husband of Napoleon's
shrew sister, Caroline   Bonaparte.   The emperor,
after conquering the separate Italian states, had
placed his ex-waiter brother-in-law on the Neapolitan
throne.

When Jeanne reached Naples, Queen Caroline received her with open arms and invited her to be a
guest at the palace.   Murat's admiration for the lovely
visitor was undisguisable.   And—though it has been
denied by one biographer that Jeanne was responsible
for his treason—almost at once after her arrival, he
began to intrigue with Napoleon's enemies.   Form
your own conclusions, as did folk of the time.

Soon afterward, weakened by the idiotic Russian
campaign, Napoleon was set upon by a host of foes.
Men who had licked his boots fell over one another
to join the alliance against him.

The lion was wounded, and the dog pack was at
his throat.

As soon as Napoleon had been hustled off into exile,
the Recamiers returned to Paris, as did practically all
the army of people he had banished.   The banker's
fortune was looking up, and they could live in something of their old style there.

Paris, in those first weeks of the "Restoration," was
as full of kings, emperors, princes, and dukes as a subway rush-hour train of newspaper readers.   One could

hardly walk a block without stumbling over a monarch or a commander-in-chief or a princeling.

The heads of the allied armies were still there, strutting gallantly about—they would have run up a tree, two years earlier—and bragging of Napoleon's fall.

There was Alexander, Czar of Russia, gigantic and bearlike, who had once cringed to Napoleon, then frozen and starved him in the Moscow campaign, and now was one of the chiefs of the alliance. There, too, was Blucher, who had tumbled off his horse at Waterloo, but who, none the less, had done more than is placed to his credit to win the victory that forever crushed Napoleon. It was he and his Prussians, not Wellington and the English, who really won Waterloo for the Allies.

Other sovereigns, other generals, there were, too. And, foremost among them, a long, lean Irishman, with a bony face and a great hooked beak of a nose. He was Arthur Wellesley, Duke of Wellington, titular Victor of Waterloo and Man of the Hour.

The Duke of Wellington was not happily married. I think no retroactive libel law can attack me for saying this, for he himself made no secret of it. And he was far from being an exponent of stern British morality.

Indeed, one object of his affections, Miss Jenkins, wrote of him to a friend:

"It was all I could do to prevent His Grace from

throwing himself on his knees before me in sinful adulation."

I fear he would have roused crass horror in the bosom of the mid-Victorian matron who, on seeing Shakespeare's "Antony and Cleopatra," exclaimed:

"How different was Cleopatra's home life from that of our own gracious queen!"

The duke fell victim to Jeanne Recamier's charm. He, the official Man of the Hour, became a fixture at her salons—but for a very brief time. One day, when he was calling on her, a number of other guests being present, the duke made some would-be-witty remark about France.

Jeanne chose to interpret his words as a slur on her beloved country. Roused for once from her wonted gentleness, she ordered Wellington out of her house.

By the next day all Paris knew that Madame Recamier had shown the omnipotent Duke of Wellington the door. And all Paris—which adored Jeanne and hated the English hero—went wild with delight. Jeanne's popularity from that moment was boundless.

Soon afterward, Wellington found that stern duty called him, somewhat hastily, to London. Whither, to his disgust, the story of his ejectment from Madame Recamier's salon had preceded him.

Canova, the premier sculptor of his day—he who later paid such assiduous court to Elizabeth Patterson —fell in love with Jeanne. So indelibly was her wonder face stamped on his mind that, without her knowing it, he was able to make two busts of her.

When the busts were done, Canova who was constantly receiving and rejecting offers of fabulous sums to make portrait busts—showed her his labors of love. But Jeanne's beauty went hand in hand with vanity. She thought the busts over which he had toiled so happily did not do her justice. And without a word she turned away from the inspection and left the studio.

The sharp blow to his pride was too much for Canova. He dropped her acquaintance forever; being perhaps the only one of Jeanne's adorers to break his allegiance to her before she gave the word.

Recamier died. Jeanne, rich and still gloriously beautiful, received shoals of proposals. She rejected them all. She had at last met the love of her life. In the lives of all these super-women, you will have noticed, there was some one man who stood out supreme above all the host of lesser lovers; idolized, placed on a lofty pedestal, a wealth of devotion lavished on him.

And so it was with Jeanne Recamier—although the affair from first to last was starkly platonic. She who had laughed at an emperor, who had rejected a prince's hand, who had turned the most famous man in Europe out of her house, lost her head and her heart to a cranky, bearlike author-adventurer, Francois Auguste de Chateaubriand. Your grandmother read and wept over his American novel, "Atala."

Chateaubriand was a heartbreaker. As a mere

youth, his talent for transferring his allegiance with lightning speed from one woman to the next had won for him the sobriquet "L'Inconstant." He had traveled in the American wilderness, living among Indian tribes; had hobnobbed with George Washington, to whom he had brought letters of introduction; had been sent fleeing for his life from France during the Terror; had been a favorite of Napoleon's until the Corsican's tyranny disgusted him into turning conspirator.

Of late years he had wandered aimlessly about Europe, making love and earning a scant living as a painter and writer. Sometimes broke, sometimes flush, sometimes acclaimed as a genius, sometimes chased as a political criminal, sometimes in palaces, sometimes in jail—Chateaubriand at length met Jeanne Recamier.

From the first they loved each other. On neither side was it a crazily passionate adoration. Rather was it the full, calm devotion of mature hearts that seek safe harbor after many and battering storms.

When Recamier died, Chateaubriand formally asked Jeanne's hand in marriage. She refused—for reasons best known to herself and her physician. But they remained, for all the rest of their lives, faithful and utterly devoted lovers.

Chateaubriand was uncouth, morbid, vain, bristling with a myriad foibles and faults. Jeanne, very gently and tactfully, undertook to cure him of these defects. With tender hands she gradually remolded his wayward, eccentric nature, stripping away much of its dross, bringing out its cleaner, nobler traits.

"You have transformed my character," he wrote her. "I know nothing more beautiful nor more good than you."

When Recamier died, in 1830, Jeanne was a little over fifty. Chateaubriand was sixty-two. A mature couple, withal. Yet Jeanne looked scarce thirty, and Chateaubriand was still in his late prime.

Again and again he pleaded with Jeanne to marry him. Always she refused, just as she refused a host of others, even in her mature years. Indeed, she received and rejected a proposal of marriage when she was seventy.

The rest of this story is not especially romantic. Perhaps it may not interest you. For it has to do with "the breaking up of things."

The Recamier-Chateaubriand affair went on like an Indian summer, for years. Then, as old age reached out for him, Chateaubriand's eccentricities cropped out afresh. He fell into a melancholy, shut himself away from the world that was at last growing to honor him, became a recluse, and would see no one except Madame Recamier.

His melancholy deepened almost into mania. He had but one dream of life left in his heart—his love for Jeanne. To her he clung like a frightened child to a tender mother.

Then, in its saddest form, old age laid its cold hand

across beautiful Jeanne's orange-tinted eyes, and she became totally blind. Even in her blindness she was still lovely, and her soul lost none of its sweetness.

Sightless, she still guarded and sought to amuse the cranky old man she so long had loved; bearing with his once-imperious temper, which had now rotted into mere whining discontent; humoring his million whims; talking softly to him, in his brighter moments, about the gleaming past.

The melancholy old man, lovingly tended and nursed and amused like a baby by the blind old woman who had been the reigning beauty of the world, lingered on for several years longer.

When at last he died, Jeanne mourned him as never had she mourned Recamier or any other. Chateaubriand's death broke her heart. It broke, too, her last tie to earth. And within a few months she followed her lover to the grave.

Thus, at seventy-two, died Jeanne Recamier, virgin heartbreaker, whose very name was for half a century the synonym for absolute beauty and flawless purity. I know of no other super-woman whose character in any way resembles hers.

Which was, perhaps, more unlucky for the other super-women than for the men who loved them.

CHAPTER XII

LADY HAMILTON

PATRON SAINT OF DIME-NOVEL HEROINES

SHE was the mother of Gertrude the Governess, the granddam of Bertha the Beautiful Sewing-machine Girl, the earliest ancestorette of Ione, the Pride of the Mill; she was the impossibility that made possible the brain daughters of Laura Jean. She was the patron saint of all the dime-novel heroines; she was the model, conciously or otherwise—probably otherwise—of all their authors. Because, at a period when such things were undreamed of, even in fiction, she rose from nursemaid to title.

Even in the books and plays of that age, the born serving wench did not marry the heir. In the highest literary flights, Bridget's crowning reward was to wed Luke, the gamekeeper, and become landlady of The Bibulous Goat or The Doodlethorpe Arms. Goldsmith was eyed askance for even making the heroine of "She Stoops to Conquer" pose momentarily as a lady's maid.

Having thus tried to show how impossible was the

happening, let me work up by degrees to the happening itself.

She was a Lancashire lass, Emma Lyon by name. In mature years she dropped the "Lyon" and called herself "Emma Harte." No one knows why. Lyon was not her name; neither was Harte, for that matter. In fact, she had no name; her careless parents having failed to supply her with the legal right to one.

Her father was a rural farm hand. He died while Emma was a baby. Her mother, an inn servant, moved later to Hawarden; and there a Mrs. Thomas hired Emma as nursemaid. This was in 1777. Emma was thirteen. She had already learned to read—a rare accomplishment in those days for the nameless brat of an inn drudge. And, as nursemaid, she greedily picked up stray morsels of her little charges' education, as well as the manners and language of her employers. She learned as quickly as a Chinaman.

There is a hiatus in the records, after Emma had served a year or so in the Thomas family. One biographer bridges the gap with a line of asterisks. Asterisks, in biographies as well as in sex-problem fiction, may indicate either a lapse of time or a lapse of morals.

Emma reappeared from the asterisk cloud in London, where she was nursemaid in the house of a Doctor Budd, one of the physicians at St. Bartholomew's Hospital. Doctor Budd's housemaid at that time, by the way, later became a Drury Lane star, under the name of "Mrs. Powell." And in that bright afterday she and the even more apotheosized Emma renewed their below-stairs friendship.

For some reason Emma left Doctor Budd's service rather suddenly and found a job as helper in the shop of a St. James' Market mercer. She was sixteen, and she was gloriously beautiful. Her figure was superb. Already she had a subtle charm of her own which drew to her feet crowds of footmen, shopboys, apprentices, and such small deer. There is no record that they one and all were sent away disconsolate.

During her brief career as helper to the St. James' Market mercer, Emma chanced to attract the notice of a woman of quality who one day entered the shop. And forthwith she was hired as lady's maid. The girl had picked up a smattering of education. She had scraped from her pink tongue the rough Lancashire bur-r-r. She had learned to speak correctly, to ape the behavior of the solid folk whose servant she had been. Now, from her new employer, she was to learn at firsthand how people in the world of fashion comported themselves. And, chameleonlike, she took on the color of her gay surroundings.

Soon she could lisp such choice and fashionable expletives as "Scrape me raw!" and "Oh, lay me bleeding!" and could talk and walk and posture as did her mistress. Trashy novels by the dozen fell into her hands from her mistress' table. Emma devoured them gluttonously and absorbed their precepts as the human system absorbs alcohol fumes.

Please don't for one moment get the idea that there was anything profitable to a young girl in the novels of the latter eighteenth century. Perhaps you have in mind such dreary sterling works as "Pamela," "Clarissa Harlowe," "Sir Charles Grandison," and others that were crammed into your miserably protesting brain in the Literature Courses. Those were the rare—the very rare—exceptions to a large and lurid list, which included such choice classics as "Moll Flanders," "Roxana"—both of them by the same Defoe who wrote "Robinson Crusoe," and whose other novels would send a present-day publisher to States prison—"Peregrine Pickle," "Fanny Hill," "The Delicate Distress," "Roderick Random," and the rest of a rank-flavored multitude.

Emma reveled in the joys of the local "circulating library," too: one of those places that loaned books of a sort to cause even the kindly Sheridan to thunder his famous dictum:

"A circulating library in a town is an evergreen tree of diabolical knowledge. It blossoms through the year. And, depend on't, they who are so fond of handling the leaves will long for the fruit at last."

Much reading filled Emma with wonderful new ideas of life. Incidentally, it made her neglect her work, and she was discharged. Her next step was to become barmaid in a tavern. While she was there, a young admirer of hers was seized by the navy press gang. Emma went to the captain of the ship to beg for her swain's release. The captain was John Willett Payne, afterward a rear admiral. Payne granted the lovely girl's plea. He not only gave her what she asked, but his own admiration as well. Her story as a heart winner had begun.

In fiction, the gallant captain would soon have tired of his lively sweetheart and cast her aside. But Emma was not a lowly sweetheart. She was a super-woman. She showed how much stranger than fiction truth may be by deserting Payne for a richer man. First, however, she had wheedled the captain into hiring tutors and music masters for her, and she profited vastly by their teachings.

Her new flame was a sporting baronet, Sir Harry Featherstonhaugh, of Up Park, Sussex. Sir Harry was an all-round athlete and a reckless horseman. He taught Emma to ride—"a beggar on horseback?"— and she became the most daring equestrienne of the century. He taught her to spend money, too. And so splendidly did she learn her lesson that inside of a year Sir Harry was bankrupt.

Perhaps **all** rats do not leave a sinking ship; but, for very good reasons, one never hears anything further of the rats that don't. The rat that wishes to continue his career wastes no time in joining the exodus. And Emma Lyon did not disdain to take example from the humble rodent.

There seemed no good reason for remaining longer at the side of the bankrupt baronet, to add to his cares and expenses. So, with womanly consideration, she left him.

She was alone in the world once more, without a shilling or a friend; equipped with education, accomplishments, wondrous beauty, and charm, but with no immediate market for those commodities. It was the black hour that comes at least once into the life of every adventuress.

And, in this time of need, she fell in with a beauty-culture quack, Graham by name.

Graham had devised a rejuvenation medicine—from Doctor Faustus down, the world has feverishly, piteously seized on every nostrum advertised as a means of exchanging age for youth—and he vowed that it would make its users not only young again, but maddeningly beautiful. As an example of "after using," Graham exhibited Emma Lyon, who, he said, had once been old and ugly, and who, by a course of his elixir, had become youthful and glorious. He called his medicine "Megalanthropogenesis." Women who heard his lecture took one look at Emma and then bought out Graham's ready supply of the stuff. The charlatan was an artist in gaining his effects, as witness a report of the exhibition in which Emma posed:

He had contrived a "Bed of Apollo," or "Celestial Bed," on which, in a delicately colored light, this exquisitely beautiful woman, nearly naked, was gradually unveiled, to soft, soft music, as Hygeia, goddess of health.

Presumably no effort was made by any eighteenth-century Comstock to suppress this show, and all London flocked and thronged and jostled to behold it. Apart from the normal crowd of idlers, came painters and sculptors to gaze in delight on the perfect face and form revealed through the shimmer of rose-colored light.

And foremost of these artists was a freakish genius toward whom was slowly creeping the insanity that a few years later was to claim him, and whose stealthy approach he was even then watching with horror. He was George Romney, who, with Sir Joshua Reynolds, divided the homage of England's art world. Romney had come to stare at Emma. He remained to worship. He engaged her as his model, and, soon or late, painted no less than thirty-nine pictures of her.

"I call her 'The Divine Lady,' " he once wrote. "For I think she is superior to all womankind."

The black hour was past. Emma Lyon's fortune and fame were secure. Thanks to Romney, she was the best-advertised beauty on earth. Conquests came thick and fast, not treading on one another's heels, but racing abreast.

Soon, out of the ruck and forging far ahead, appeared Charles Francis Greville, wit, art connoisseur, and nephew and heir of the famed antiquary diplomat, Sir William Hamilton. Greville cut out all rivals, Romney among the rest, and won Emma for his own.

Theirs was an odd love affair. For here, too, Emma

gave full rein to her craving for education.   And
she showed for the first time just why she was so eager
to be highly educated.   It was not for mere learning's
sake, but to enhance the charm that gave her a hold
over men.   She cared nothing for any but the showy
accomplishments.   She already had a fair groundwork
in English and ordinary school studies.   She made
Greville get her the best teachers in singing, in dancing, in acting.   Perhaps she looked forward to a stage
triumph, but more likely to outshining the colorless
bread-and-butter women of her day.

Never did pupil better repay the pains of her
teachers.   Her voice presently rivaled that of many a
prima donna.   Her dancing was a delight.   It was she
who conceived the celebrated "shawl dance" that was
the rage throughout Europe for years thereafter, and
that still is used, in very slightly modified form, by
premieres danseuses.   But acting was Emma's forte.
Says a contemporary writer:

> With a common piece of stuff she could so arrange and
> clothe herself as to offer the most appropriate representations
> of a Jewess, a Roman matron, a Helen, Penelope, or Aspasia.
> No character seemed foreign to her, and the grace she was
> in the habit of displaying under such representations excited the
> admiration of all who were fortunate enough to be present on
> such occasions.   Siddons could not surpass the grandeur of her
> style or O'Neil be more melting in the utterance of deep pathos.

In this heyday of her prosperity, Emma hunted up

her aged and disreputable mother, bestowed on her the name "Mrs. Cadogan," and settled a rich pension on her. At about the same time, too, Emma bade a cheery farewell to the serviceable name of Lyon and took to calling herself Emma Harte.

Then Greville went broke.

In his new-found poverty, he hit on a plan of life foreign to all his old ideas.

He decided to ask his rich old uncle, Sir William Hamilton, to pay his debts and settle a little annuity on him. With his sum as a means of livelihood, he intended to marry Emma, and, with her and their three children, settle down in some cheap suburb.

How this appealed to Emma history forgets to say. Judging by both past and future, it is not unjust to suppose that she may have been making ready once more to emulate the ship-deserting rat. But this time she did not need to. The ship was about to desert her —for a consideration.

Greville, full of his new hopes, went to Sir William Hamilton and laid the plan before him. His nephew's derelictions from the straight and narrow path had long distressed the virtuous old diplomat. And in Greville's financial troubles Sir William thought he saw a fine chance to break off his nephew's discreditable affair with Emma.

He offered to set Greville on his feet again if that luckless youth would drop Emma's acquaintance. The enamored Greville refused. Sir William insisted, raising his offer of financial aid, and pointing out, with tearful eloquence, the family disgrace that a marriage to a woman of Emma's dissolute character must cause. It was all quite like a scene from a modern problem play. But Fate, her tongue in her cheek, was preparing to put a twist on the end of the scene worthy of the most cynical French vaudeville writer.

Greville resented his uncle's rash judgment of his adored Emma, and begged him to come and see her for himself, hoping that Emma's wonder charm might soften the old man's virtue-incrusted heart. Reluctantly, Sir William consented to one brief interview with the wicked siren.

At sight of Emma, Sir William's heart melted to mushiness. He fell crazily in love with the woman he had come to dispossess. There was another long and stormy scene between uncle and nephew; after which Greville, for an enormous lump sum, transferred to Sir William Hamilton all right and title and good will to the adorable Emma Harte. And Sir William and Emma departed thence, arm in arm, leaving Greville a sadder but a richer man. What became of the three children I don't know. By the way, Emma had taught them to call her "aunt," not "mother."

Will you let me quote a deadly dry line or two from an encyclopedia, to prove to you how important a personage Sir William was, and how true is the axiom about "no fool like an old fool"?

Hamilton, Sir William, British diplomatist and antiquary
(1730-1803), student of art, philosophy and literature. From
1764 to 1800 English ambassador to the Court of Naples.
Trustee of British Museum, Fellow of the Royal Society, vice
president of the Society of Antiquaries, distinguished member
of the Dilettante Club, author of several books. Sir Joshua
Reynolds, his intimate friend, painted his portrait, which hangs
in the National Gallery.

Sir William, who was home on leave of absence when
he met Emma, took her back with him to Italy. But
before they sailed she had prevailed on him to marry
her.

It was easy. He was old.

The marriage was kept secret until, in 1791, she led
her husband back to England on another leave of absence and up to the altar of St. George's Church, where,
on September 6th of that year, they were married all
over again; this time with every atom of publicity
Emma could compass. She was then twenty-seven; her
husband was sixty-one.

In state they returned to the court of Naples—the
most corrupt, licentious, false, utterly abominable court
in all Europe. If you will glance at the annals of the
courts of that period you will find this statement is as
true as it is sweeping. On her earlier visit, as the supposed brevet bride of the ambassador, Emma had been
warmly received by Marie Caroline, Queen of Naples
and sister to Marie Antoinette of France. Emma and
Marie Caroline were kindred spirits—which is perhaps

the unkindest thing I could say about either of them—
and they quickly formed a lasting friendship for each
other.

Emma was glad to get back to Naples. Apart from
her marriage, her visit to England had not been a success. A certain element in London society, attracted
by her beauty, her voice, and her talent as an actress,
had taken her up. But Queen Charlotte had refused her
a presentation at the British court, and the more reputable element of the nobility had followed royal example
and given her a wide berth. English society under
George III. was severely respectable—at least in the
matter of externals; a quality it was soon to mislay,
under George IV. Hence Emma's joy at returning to
a court where respectability was a term to be found
only in the dictionary.

The King of Naples was a fool. His wife was the
little kingdom's ruler. Emma, Lady Hamilton, became
her chief adviser. Writes one historian:

It is not too much to say of these two women that for
years they wielded the destinies of Naples, and seriously affected the character of the wars that ended with the peace of
Europe in 1815, when both were dead. . . . Both were
endowed with powers of mind far above the average of their
sex; both exhibited energy and understanding that inspired them
to bold and decisive, if not always laudable, deeds; both were
as remarkable for their personal beauty as for their self-reli-
ance, their knowledge of men, and their determination to make
the most of their information. To say that Marie Caroline
loved Lady Hamilton is to misstate a fact; there was no love in

the royal composition; but her ungovernable and undying hatred of the French inclined her, no doubt, in the first instance toward the wife of the English ambassador, and the subsequent devotion of the favorite secured an attachment that is confessed and reiterated through whole pages of a vehement and overstrained correspondence.

Naples, just then, was between two fires. There was fear of a French invasion—which arrived on schedule time—and there was also danger that England would ruin Neapolitan commerce. Emma's white hands were at once plunged, wrist-deep, into the political dough; and a sorry mess she proceeded to make of it. For example, the King of Spain wrote a confidential letter to his brother, the King of Naples, accusing the English government of all sorts of public and private crimes and telling of Spain's secret alliance with France. The king showed it to his wife, who in turn showed it to Lady Hamilton. Emma stole and secretly sent the letter to the British cabinet. The result was a bloody war between England and Spain.

About two years after Emma's marriage, an English warship, the **Agamemnon,** touched at Naples, and her captain called to pay his respects to the British ambassador and to deliver a letter from the admiral of the Mediterranean fleet. After a few minutes' talk with the captain, Sir William insisted that the latter should meet Lady Hamilton.

He bustled into the drawing-room to prepare Emma for the visitor's arrival, saying excitedly to her:

"I am bringing you a little man who cannot boast of being very handsome, but who, I pronounce, will one day astonish the world. I know it from the very words of conversation I have had with him."

On the heels of Sir William's announcement, the "little man" came into the room. At first glance, he scarcely seemed to justify Hamilton's enthusiasm. He was clad in a full-laced uniform. His lank, unpowdered hair was tied in a stiff Hessian queue of extraordinary length. Old-fashioned, flaring waistcoat flaps added to the general oddity of his figure.

Sir William introduced him as "Captain Horatio Nelson."

Lady Hamilton lavished on the queer guest no especial cordiality. It is not known that she gave him a second thought. Nelson, little more impressed by the super-woman, wrote to his wife in England an account of the call, saying of Lady Hamilton—whose story, of course, he and everybody knew:

"She is a young woman of amiable manners, who does honor to the station to which she has been raised."

Yet Nelson had unwittingly met the woman who was to tarnish the pure glory of his fame; and Emma had met the man but for whom she would today be forgotten. So little does Fate forecast her dramas that, at the first meeting, neither of the two immortal lovers seems to have felt any attraction for the other.

Not for five busy years did Nelson and Emma Hamilton see each other again.

Then Nelson came back to Naples, this time in triumph—a world-renowned hero, the champion of the seas, Britain's idol. He had become an admiral, a peer of England, a scourge of his country's foes. Back to Naples he came. Part of him; not all—for victorious warfare had set cruel marks on him. He had left his right eye at Calvi in 1794, and his right arm at Teneriffe in 1797. He was more odd looking than ever, but he was an acclaimed hero. And Naples in general and Emma Hamilton in particular welcomed him with rapture.

He was in search of the French fleet, and he wanted the King of Naples to let him reprovision his ships in the Neapolitan harbor. Now, France and Naples just then happened to be at peace. And, by their treaty, no more than two English warships at a time could enter any Neapolitan or Sicilian port. The king's council declared the treaty must stand. Lady Hamilton decided otherwise.

She used all her power with the queen to have the treaty set aside. As a result Marie Caroline issued an order directing "all governors of the two Sicilies to water, victual, and aid" Nelson's fleet. This order made it possible for Nelson to go forth reprovisioned— and to crush the French in the Battle of the Nile.

In the first rumor of this battle that reached Naples, Nelson was reported killed. Soon afterward he appeared, alive and well, in the harbor. Here is his letter to his wife, telling how Lady Hamilton received him on his return. Nelson, by the way. had been married for nearly twelve years. He and his wife were devoted to each other. Judging from this letter, he was lamentably ignorant of women or was incredibly sure of Lady Nelson's love and trust. Or else his courage was greater than that of mortal husband. He wrote:

> Sir William and Lady Hamilton came out to sea to meet me. They, my most respectable friends, had nearly been laid up and seriously ill, first from anxiety and then from joy. It was imprudently told Lady Hamilton, in a moment, that I was alive; and the effect was like a shot. She fell, apparently dead, and is not yet perfectly recovered from severe bruises. Alongside came my honored friends. The scene in the boat was terribly affecting. Up flew her ladyship, and, exclaiming: "Oh, God, is it possible?" she fell into my arm, more dead than alive. Tears, however, soon set matters to rights; when alongside came the king. . . . I hope, some day, to have the pleasure of introducing you to Lady Hamilton. She is one of the very best women in the world; she is an honor to her sex. Her kindness, with Sir William's, to me, is more than I can express. I am in their house, and I may tell you, it required all the kindness of my friends to set me up. Lady Hamilton intends writing to you. May God Almighty bless you, and give us in due time a happy meeting!

France sought revenge for the help given to Nelson's fleet, and declared war on Naples. The Neapolitans, in fury at being dragged into such a needless conflict, rose against their dear king and adored queen—especially against their adored queen—and threatened to kill them. By Lady Hamilton's aid the royal family

reached Nelson's flagship and took refuge there from
the mob.   Sir William and Lady Hamilton went along.
The populace looted the British embassy and stole
everything of value Sir William owned—about one
hundred and ninety-five thousand dollars' worth of
property in all.   Thus, Hamilton was the third man
who had lost a fortune through Emma.

Meanwhile, Nelson had sailed to Palermo, taking the
fugitives along.   There he made his home with the
Hamiltons.   And scandal awoke, even in that easy-
going crowd.   Nor did the scandal die down to any
appreciable extent on the birth of Lady Hamilton's
daughter, Horatia, a year or so later.

Sir William's conduct in the matter is still a puzzle.
He felt, or professed to feel, that there was no occasion
for jealousy.   And so for a long time the trio shared
the same house.

One of the courtiers who had fled with the king and
queen to Palermo was Prince Caraccioli, Nelson's close
friend and Lady Hamilton's bitter enemy.   Caraccioli
asked leave to go back to Naples to look after his en-
dangered property.   As soon as he reached the city,
he threw in his lot with the rebels and was made admiral of their navy.

Presently, by the aid of England's fleet, the royal
family returned.   The rebellion was put down, and the
king and queen were once more seated firmly on their
thrones.   The rebel leaders were seized and brought to
trial.   Nelson is said to have promised immunity to

Caraccioli if he would surrender. Relying on his friend's pledge, Caraccioli surrendered. At Emma's request Nelson had the overtrustful man hanged from the yardarm of his own flagship.

This is the darkest smear on Nelson's character, a smear that even his most blatant admirers have never been able to wipe away. It is not in keeping with anything else in his life. But by this time he belonged to Lady Hamilton, body and soul.

She, by the way, had managed to acquire from her friend, the Queen of Naples, a nice tendency toward blood-thirstiness; as witness the following sweet anecdote by Pryne Lockhart Gordon, who tells of dining with the Hamiltons at Palermo, in company with a Turkish officer:

> In the course of conversation, the officer boasted that with the sword he wore he had put to death a number of French prisoners. "Look," he said, "there is their blood remaining on it." When the speech was translated to her, Lady Hamilton's eyes beamed with delight. "Oh, let me see the sword that did the glorious deed!" she exclaimed. Taking the sword in her hands, which were covered with jewels, she looked at it, then kissed the incrusted blood on the blade, and passed it on to Nelson. Only one who was a witness to the spectacle can imagine how disgusting it was.

Enshrined once more at Naples, hailed as savior of the realm, acclaimed for her share in the Nile victory, the confidante of royalty—it would be pleasant to say good-by here to Emma Lyon, ex-nursemaid, ex-bar-

maid, ex-lady's maid, nameless offspring of a Lancashire inn slavey. It was the climax of a wonderful
life. But there was anti-climax aplenty to follow.

Nelson went home to England to receive the plaudits
of his fellow countrymen and to settle accounts with
his wife. Home, too, came the Hamiltons, Sir William
having been recalled.

Lady Nelson was not at the dock to meet her hero
husband. Bad news traveled fast, even before we
boosted it along by wire and then by wireless. Lady
Nelson had heard. And Lady Nelson was waiting at
home. Thither, blithely enough, fared the man in
whose praise a million Englishmen were cheering themselves hoarse—and in whose silver-buckled shoes perhaps no married Englishman would just then have
cared or dared to stand. But Nelson was a hero. He
went home.

I once had a collie puppy that had never chanced
to be at close quarters with a cat. I was privileged to
see him when he made his first gleefully fearless attack
upon one, ignorant of the potential anguish tucked
away behind a feline's velvety paws. Somehow—with
no disrespect to a great man—I always think of that
poor, about-to-be-disillusioned puppy when I try to
visualize the picture of Nelson's home-coming.

Just what happened no one knows. But whatever
it was, it did not teach Nelson the wisdom of husbandly
reticence. For, a few weeks later, he remarked at
breakfast:

"I have just received another letter from dear Lady Hamilton."

"I am sick of hearing of 'dear' Lady Hamilton!" flared the long-suffering wife. "You can choose between us. You must give up her or me."

"Take care, Fanny!" warned Nelson. "I love you dearly. But I cannot forget all I owe to dear Lady Hamilton."

"This is the end, then," announced Lady Nelson, and she left the house.

Only once again did she and her husband meet.

Nelson cast off all pretense at concealment after his wife left him. His affair with Lady Hamilton became public property. Their daughter, Horatia, was openly acclaimed by him as his heiress. The English were in a quandary. They loved Nelson; they hated the woman who had dragged his name into the filth. They could not snub her without making him unhappy; they could not honor him without causing her to shine by reflected glory. It was unpleasant all around.

In 1805 the deadlock was broken. Nelson was again to fight the French. He told Lady Hamilton and many others that this campaign was to end in his death. He ordered his coffin made ready for him. Then he sailed against the French fleet, met it off Cape Trafalgar, and annihilated it. In the thick of the fight a musket ball gave him his death wound. He was carried below, and there, the battle raging around him, he laboriously wrote a codicil to his will, entreating his king and country to repay his services by settling a pension on Lady Hamilton. Then to his next-in-command he panted:

"I am going fast. Come nearer. Pray let my dear Lady Hamilton have my hair and all other things belonging to me. Take care of my dear Lady Hamilton —poor Lady Hamilton! Thank God I have done my duty!"

And so he died, this knightly little demigod—true lover, false husband—who had fouled his snowy escutcheon for a worthless woman.

Now comes the inevitable anticlimax.

All England turned with loathing from Lady Hamilton. Her husband was dead. Lovers stood aloof. Folk who had received her for Nelson's sake barred their doors against her. She had followed the popular custom of living in luxury on nothing a year. Now her creditors swarmed upon her.

Her house was sold for debt. Next she lived in Bond Street lodgings. growing poorer day by day until she was condemned to the debtor's prison. A kind-hearted —or hopeful—alderman bought her out of jail. A former coachman of hers, whose wages were still unpaid, threatened her with arrest for debt. She fled to Calais.

There she lived in an attic, saved from absolute starvation by a fellow Englishwoman, a Mrs. Hunter. Her youth and charm had fled. The power that had lured Nelson and Greville and Hamilton to ruin was gone.

In 1815 she died. She was buried in a pine box,

with an old black silk petticoat for a pall.   No clergyman could be found to take charge of her funeral. So
the burial service was read by a fellow debt exile—a
half-pay Irish army captain.

One wonders—perhaps morbidly—if Nelson's possible punishment in another world might not have been
the knowledge of what befell his "dear" Lady Hamilton in her latter days.

THE END.

CPSIA information can be obtained
at www.ICGtesting.com
Printed in the USA
BVHW081745260819
556835BV00022B/3603/P

9 781162 785257